UNDERSTANDING
MAXINE HONG KINGSTON

UNDERSTANDING CONTEMPORARY AMERICAN LITERATURE

Matthew J. Bruccoli, Founding Editor

Linda Wagner-Martin, Series Editor

UNDERSTANDING

MAXINE HONG KINGSTON

Julia H. Lee

The University of South Carolina Press

Published by the University of South Carolina Press
Columbia, South Carolina 29208

www.sc.edu/uscpress

Manufactured in the United States of America

27 26 25 24 23 22 21 20 19 18 10 9 8 7 6 5 4 3 2 1

Library of Congress Cataloging-in-Publication Data
can be found at http://catalog.loc.gov/.

ISBN: 978-1-61117-853-1 (hardcover)
ISBN: 978-1-61117-854-8 (ebook)

This book was printed on recycled paper with
30 percent postconsumer waste content.

For Philip, Eleanor, and Silas

CONTENTS

SERIES EDITOR'S PREFACE

The Understanding Contemporary American Literature series was founded by the estimable Matthew J. Bruccoli (1931–2008), who envisioned these volumes as guides or companions for students as well as good nonacademic readers, a legacy that will continue as new volumes are developed to fill in gaps among the nearly one hundred series volumes published to date and to embrace a host of new writers only now making their marks on our literature.

As Professor Bruccoli explained in his preface to the volumes he edited, because much influential contemporary literature makes special demands, "the word understanding in the titles was chosen deliberately. Many willing readers lack an adequate understanding of how contemporary literature works; that is, of what the author is attempting to express and the means by which it is conveyed." Aimed at fostering this understanding of good literature and good writers, the criticism and analysis in the series provide instruction in how to read certain contemporary writers—explicating their material, language, structures, themes, and perspectives—and facilitate a more profitable experience of the works under discussion.

In the twenty-first century Professor Bruccoli's prescience gives us an avenue to publish expert critiques of significant contemporary American writing. The series continues to map the literary landscape and to provide both instruction and enjoyment. Future volumes will seek to introduce new voices alongside canonized favorites, to chronicle the changing literature of our times, and to remain, as Professor Bruccoli conceived, contemporary in the best sense of the word.

Linda Wagner-Martin, Series Editor

ACKNOWLEDGMENTS

My deepest thanks to Linda Wagner-Martin, who recognized the need for a volume on Maxine Hong Kingston and was as supportive an editor as one could wish for. She has been a mentor to me since my first days in graduate school, and I'm delighted to have this chance to thank her for the counsel and support she has provided to me and other women of color academics over the years. I also thank Jennifer Ho at the University of North Carolina, Chapel Hill, for making me aware of this opportunity and providing useful advice on the process; she is a valued colleague and friend. Jim Denton and his colleagues at the University of South Carolina Press have shepherded this text through various stages with a good humor and patience. Over the past fifteen years, my students at the University of California at Los Angeles, the University of Texas at Austin, and the University of California at Irvine have made reading Maxine Hong Kingston a joyful, maddening, and thought-provoking experience. I thank them for the enthusiasm, cynicism, confusion, and wonder with which they have approached her words.

CHAPTER 1

Understanding Maxine Hong Kingston

Maxine Hong Kingston once stated that her contribution to literature was showing "how to get from the oral to the written."[1] Her career has been defined by her attempts to write down the "huge inheritance of talk story" that her ancestors have passed down from one family member to the next, from one generation to another, over the years.[2] Committing these stories to the page has been no easy task, for as she reveals in her works, these talk-stories change—sometimes subtly, sometimes dramatically—with each retelling, and Kingston's own memory of these stories and her re-imagining of them impact the form the textual versions take. And yet, she is deeply attentive to keeping alive in her own text the dissent between the oral versions: the contradictions, inconsistencies, and idiosyncrasies that make it impossible to authenticate the stories or impose a unified logic to them. This is what Kingston means when she talks of getting "from the oral to the written"—the process of writing for her is not about codifying any one version of a story so much as acknowledging the multiplicity of stories that make up the history of her family's experiences.

The story of Maxine Hong Kingston's own life will sound familiar to those who have read *The Woman Warrior, China Men,* or her other works, for she revisits scenes from her past frequently in her writing. Her childhood in Stockton, her complicated relationship with her parents, the Chinatown in which she grew up, and the histories—both national and familial—that brought her parents as well as thousands of others from China to Chinatown proved to be fertile ground for generating the narratives that form the backbone of her literary career. After the publication of *China Men* in 1980, Kingston claimed that she had "told all my childhood stories," and at first glance, this statement seems to be an accurate one, since her subsequent works do not seem to mine her own childhood for source materials in the same way that *The Woman Warrior* and *China Men* do. And yet, the experiences of her family and the Chinese American community—its politics, histories, losses, and triumphs—are a deeply essential part of all of Kingston's writing, even as she has experimented with genres, forms, and language.

Life and Career

Maxine Ting Ting Hong was born in Stockton, California, on October 27, 1940. Her parents were Tom and Ying Lan Hong. Before coming to the United States, Kingston's father was a teacher and scholar in his home village of Sun Woi (New Society Village) in Guangzhou. Like thousands of other Chinese men before him, he left his home and young family in 1924 in order to seek out the wealth and prosperity that Gold Mountain promised. In *China Men,* the narrator suggests that her father left China for the United States as much out of boredom and disappointment with teaching as for the financial incentives working in the United States offered. Kingston's father would have had plenty of advice on how to travel to the United States as a paper son, since he was from a family in which the men often went abroad to work before returning to China. Kingston's own grandfather, father, great-uncles, and uncles, often journeyed to the United States in search of employment. Much later in her life, Kingston's mother told her that Tom attempted to enter the United States three times via Cuba; the first two times he was caught and shipped back before he ultimately succeeded on his third attempt. Perhaps this explains why Tom never attempted to return to China once he made it into America—the chances of being turned away again were simply too high. Thus, while most of his family members traveled back and forth between Sun Woi and Gold Mountain, Tom did not.

Once in the United States, Tom Hong worked multiple jobs in order to survive: washing windows, waiting tables, and working at a laundry. These activities did not stop him from enjoying himself and all the opportunities that his new home had to offer: he socialized with other Chinese men, danced at nightclubs, flirted with white women, and toured New York like a tourist, sending back to his wife pictures of himself in his sharp and stylish Western clothes. After a number of years, he invested in a laundry with three other Chinese immigrants. At that point, Tom sent for his wife Ying Lan in China, and she joined him in 1939.

Like her husband, Ying Lan Chew, Kington's mother, was a well-educated professional in China. She and Tom had had two children in China before he decided to give up his scholarly career and try his luck on Gold Mountain.

These two children—a boy and a girl—passed away some time after his departure.[3] Casting about for something to do, Ying Lan decided to follow her husband's suggestion to learn a vocation; using the money he sent her every month, she enrolled at the To Keung School of Midwifery in Canton to train to be a doctor and midwife. She worked for a number of years in this capacity before leaving for the United States to rejoin her husband. She arrived in the United States via Angel Island in California and then traveled by train across the country to meet her husband in New York City. (Kingston only learned that her mother entered the United States via Angel Island well after the publication of both *The Woman Warrior* and *China Men*.[4] In an interview with Paul Mandelbaum, Kingston states that for most of her life, she had "always thought [my mother] came through Ellis Island because all her stories about America start with New York."[5]) When Ying Lan arrived in New York she was forty-five, and she and her husband had been separated for fifteen years.

After being cheated by his fellow business partners out of the laundry that they had all started, Tom and Ying Lan moved to California and settled in Stockton. It was here in 1940 that Maxine was born, the first of six American-born children. While Tom ran a gambling house for a much wealthier Chinese man, Ying Lan worked many odd jobs to help support the growing family: she cooked and cleaned, picked crops in the field, and worked in a cannery. Just after World War II ended, the family were finally able to achieve a level of financial independence by opening their own business in Stockton: the New Port Laundry. As with many immigrant families, the children were expected to work at the laundry, and many of Kingston's memories of her childhood revolved around the hours before and after school spent working there. While the labor was backbreaking and the hours were long (starting at dawn and ending well past midnight), the Hongs were able to use the proceeds from their business to purchase their own home, complete with a space in the back for a garden. Along with their work in the laundry and their academic responsibilities, the children attended Chinese school in the afternoons.

Like the Hongs, the Chinese who lived in Stockton during this period hailed mostly from Sun Woi and surrounding villages.[6] Although many readers and critics have sometimes erroneously assumed that Kingston grew up in the more famous Chinatown of San Francisco, Kingston herself has always averred that the Chinese community of Stockton was very different from the Chinatown inhabitants of larger California metropolitan centers like San Francisco or Los Angeles, and her narratives of growing up in Chinatown are firmly rooted in the history and spaces of Stockton. According to Kingston, the Stockton Chinatown of her childhood was relatively small and less sharply defined geographically. It was also racially integrated. Along with Chinese, Kingston and her family lived among Mexicans and African Americans as well as Caucasians. In *China Men,* the narrator proclaims, "We lived on a special spot of the earth, Stockton, the only city on the Pacific with three railroads—the Santa Fe, Southern Pacific, and Western Pacific."[7] Stockton's position within a rail network made it a crossroads and gathering place for all kinds of people, especially those who had been uprooted, not unlike her own family. So many of Kingston's relatives lived and died in Stockton after emigrating from China that many in her family called the city "ancestral ground," a home to replace the one that they had left and then lost in China. In recreating the Chinatown of her childhood, Kingston created "a territory as convincing and as American as William Faulkner's Yoknapatawpha County, or closer to Kingston's home, John Steinbeck's California."[8]

Kingston's images of a Stockton before urban renewal tore down the section of town where her parents lived and worked are particularly evocative of a space filled with obstreperous bodies in constant motion. The homeless meandering through the streets while the Hong children walked home from school; Kingston's mother picking for edible or medicinal greens and weeds in empty lots; the family going through the trash cans of businesses and neighbors to see if they could find anything of use or value for the home or to sell; the children dragging home railway ties to use in their play at home. The places of Kingston's childhood were paved over in the 1970s, expanded, or knocked down in order to make way for shopping malls, parking lots, or other more desirable, business-friendly public spaces where the homeless, transients, and people of color were often unwelcome and excluded. But these spaces live on in Kingston's narratives.

Living in Stockton's Chinatown and surrounded by a community that hailed from the same place in China as her parents and ancestors had a formative impact on Kingston as a child and then as a woman. In *The Woman Warrior,* Kingston vividly describes the pressures of growing up under the sharp eyes of these Chinese neighbors. These "villagers" are described as being officious, oppressive, and sexist, constantly denigrating the narrator as a child because of her gender and criticizing her when she misbehaved. In other writings, Kingston takes a more mellow view of growing up in Chinatown. Despite all of these economic, educational, and cultural pressures, Kingston also remembered a childhood filled with a sense of community and neighborly activities. There were "shows to raise money for China Relief. And parades with a red flag . . . and operas, live and on film. And American films on Saturday afternoons and Hong Kong films on Sundays. Talk-stories and letters that came from China were often about what happened at the theater, how the theater became Communist, how the theaters went dark. . . . America is our country not just for work but for play."[9] While her family was enthralled by the theater and films (in *The Woman Warrior,* the narrator describes an incident in which her grandmother insists that everyone goes to the theater, even though the family knows that they will be robbed that night by a marauding band of thieves), Kingston found an outlet for her own sense of identity in writing. "I Am an American Girl" was published when she was fifteen years old, and Kingston has said that its purpose was "to assert myself as an American."[10] Her love of writing lead to a journalism scholarship at the University of California, Berkeley, where she matriculated in 1958. In an interview with the *New York Times*'s Nan Robertson, Kingston recalls that her entrance into college life was a "terrible culture shock." "The reason . . . was that for the first time she did not have her big, vital, 'exhilarating' family close around her, no matter what bad times there had been."[11]

Although the struggles of her family mirrored the experiences of many Chinese American families, Kingston has always been careful to emphasize the individual personalities of her parents and to note the ways in which her family was atypical from other Chinese immigrants. This awareness stems from the tendency of readers of ethnic memoir or fiction to normalize such texts as paradigmatic of that ethnic group's history and experience. Highlighting the fact that her family often didn't fit in within the Chinatown community also deflected the charges of exoticism leveled by Kingston's Chinese American critics. After the publication of *The Woman Warrior,* Kingston's most controversial work, Kingston asked her sister "On a range of 1 to 10, how odd do you think we were? How odd was our upbringing?" Kingston's sister responds that the oddness of the family registered as an eight in her opinion, which to Kingston "means [the family was] pretty odd, which is saying that we are not very representative."[12] By emphasizing her family's "oddness," Kingston responds to white readers who might be tempted to read *The Woman Warrior* as an ethnographic tract as well as to Chinese American charges that the book represents Chinese Americans in the most stereotypical way possible. Kingston rejects the notion that her work is representative or stereotypical.

While at Berkeley, Kingston became active in the antiwar movement, protesting American involvement in Vietnam. Kingston's commitment to peace activism would only intensify as she grew older. (Kingston was also opposed to the US invasion of Iraq and was arrested in 2003 along with Alice Walker for crossing a police cordon at the White House.[13]) She graduated from Berkeley in 1962 with a degree in English and in November of that year married Earll Kingston, an aspiring actor who had also attended Berkeley. For the next few years, Kingston worked as a teacher in the Oakland area and participated in antiwar marches. The urgency of this work was no doubt deepened by the fact that two of her brothers and a brother-in-law were drafted; another brother departed the United States for Canada to avoid the draft (*Guardian*). Firmly believing that the war in Vietnam was "a war against Asians," Kingston's antiwar activism and efforts to promote peace have been a constant throughout her adult life, something that she has talked about in countless interviews and which she has incorporated in various guises in all of her published works. As she has gotten older, in fact, her antiwar work has occupied an increasingly visible place within her literary output and efforts.[14]

By 1967, both she and Earll were feeling suffocated by Berkeley, discouraged by the despair that pervaded the antiwar movement, and alarmed by the increasing reliance of their friends and fellow protestors on drugs. Feeling the need to get out of the Berkeley bubble, Kingston, Earll, and their young son Joseph moved to Hawai'i. Hawai'i had not been the Kingstons' original destination. Initially, they had planned to relocate to the Far East and stopped in Honolulu only for a visit.[15] Any thought that they had escaped the anxieties of the war by retreating to Honolulu was quickly dashed; the unmistakable presence of the American military on the Hawaiian Islands reminded them constantly of the war that was being fought. Kingston's antiwar work continued—made even more necessary by the fact that Hawai'i was a seat of military operations—and she established herself as an English and writing teacher at various educational institutes and schools in the Honolulu area.

It was while living in Hawai'i that Kingston took her first steps toward publishing her writing. According to her timeline, Kingston started work on what would become *The Woman Warrior* in approximately 1974. (She actually wrote the final chapter of *China Men* first.) She sent the manuscript to several agents, one of whom, John Shaffner, accepted it almost immediately. Editors at Alfred A. Knopf showed interest in the book but had misgivings regarding how to market it. After deciding to categorize the book as a memoir/nonfiction rather than as a novel, Knopf published *The Woman Warrior* to almost instant acclaim in 1976. John Leonard, the influential book reviewer for the *New York Times,* was an early champion of *The Woman Warrior,* famously rhapsodizing in his review that it was "one of the best I've read in years. . . . As an account of growing up female and Chinese-American in California, in a laundry of course, it is antinostalgic. It burns the fat right out of the mind. As a dream—of the 'female avenger'—it is dizzying, elemental, a poem turned into a sword."[16] Leonard's glowing review ratcheted the public's interest in the book; the fact that Kingston had come out of nowhere to publish one of the best reviewed books of the year also piqued readers and critics alike. In his review, Leonard seemed as intrigued by Kingston's anonymity as he was by her writing, querying wonderingly at the end of his review: "Who is Maxine Hong Kingston? Nobody at Knopf seems to know. They have never laid eyes on her." That mystery wouldn't last for long, as Kingston's tiny four feet nine inch frame (according to her mother, she stopped growing at age twelve after a bout of rheumatic fever) and prematurely whitened hair soon became a familiar presence at awards ceremonies and public lectures.[17]

Accolades followed. *The Woman Warrior* was awarded the National Book Critics Circle Award for Nonfiction; it eventually was listed as one of the top ten works of nonfiction of the 1970s by *Time* Magazine. Kingston was awarded the Anisfield-Wolf Race Relations Award in 1978 for the book. In 1977, she became a visiting professor of English at the University of Hawai'i, the first in a long string of academic appointments she would take on during the next thirty years. With the success of *The Woman Warrior,* Kingston was able to give up teaching and write full time. Her next book *China Men* was eagerly anticipated and its publication cemented Kingston's status within the American literary firmament. *China Men* won the National Book Award for Nonfiction, was nominated for the National Book Critics Circle Award, and was a runner-up for a Pulitzer. Kingston was awarded a National Endowment for the Arts fellowship in 1980 and a Guggenheim Fellowship in 1982. In 1984, Kingston and her husband relocated to Los Angeles from Honolulu. Later that year, she traveled for the first time to China, visiting her parents' village in Guangzhou. On this trip, she was accompanied by such literary luminaries as Toni Morrison, Leslie Marmon Silko, and Allen Ginsberg. In 1987 she published a collection of short essays titled *Hawai'i One Summer, 1978,* a series of recollections about the decade that her family spent in Hawai'i. The same year, she and Earll left Los Angeles and moved back to the Rockridge neighborhood of Oakland.

1989 saw the publication of Kingston's first and only novel, *Tripmaster Monkey: His Fake Book.* It won the P.E.N. USA West Award in Fiction and further cemented her reputation as one of the most critically acclaimed and best-selling authors in contemporary American literature. In the meanwhile, *The Woman Warrior* had become a cultural phenomenon, reaching a new generation of readers and critics. In an interview with Shelley Fisher Fishkin conducted in 1989, Kingston revealed that *The Woman Warrior* was still a bestseller in trade paperback; in 1994, *The Woman Warrior* was produced and performed by the Berkeley Repertory Theater and the Huntington Theater Company of Boston; the following year, the Center Theater Group at the Ahmanson Theater in Los Angeles staged a production of the work. In the early 1990s, honorary doctorates recognizing Kingston's literary achievements started rolling in, and she was the subject of a documentary for KQED San Francisco. She was also named a chancellor's distinguished professor in English at UC Berkeley, returning her to the institution she had attended as an undergraduate. Recognition for her contribution to the arts and humanities have come from a variety of organizations and institutions. Kingston has won the Lila Wallace Reader's Digest Award (in 1992); the National Humanities Medal (in 1997, the same year that her mother died); the John Dos Passos Prize for Literature, and the Fred Cody Lifetime Achievement Award from the Bay Area Book Reviewers Association (both in 1998). She has also been recognized for her contribution to American Letters by the National Book Foundation (in 2008) and most recently been awarded the National Medal of Arts in 2013 by President Barack Obama.

Kingston's father died in September 1991; one month after this personal tragedy, professional misfortune struck. Kingston's home in Rockridge burned to the ground in the Oakland Hills Fire, destroying everything she owned and the manuscript for book-in-progress, tentatively titled "The Fourth Book of Peace." Later that year, she exhorted the attendees of the Modern Language Association Conference to help her write a new book, a so-called fifth book of peace. *The Fifth Book of Peace* was eventually published in 2003, the year after Kingston's book of verse *To Be the Poet,* a volume that was based on a series of lectures Kingston had given at Harvard. *To Be the Poet* signaled Kingston's move away from prose and toward poetry as her preferred form of literary expression. The wellspring for Kingston's social and political activism in her later life is Buddhism; her pursuit of peace lead her in the 1980s to organize writing workshops for US Vietnam War veterans who were attempting to cope with their experiences during that conflict. Using the award money from the Lila Wallace Reader's Digest Award, Kingston began organizing writing groups across the country. These workshops resulted in the volume *Veterans of War, Veterans of Peace,* which Kingston edited. *I Love a Broad Margin to My Life,* Kingston's seventh book, came out in 2011. Dubbed a "free-verse memoir," it reflects on "politics, love, loss, aging, history, myth, and imagination." Seventy at the time of the book's publication, Kingston has hinted that this book may be her last as the desire to write has finally ebbed slightly in her older years.[18]

Style, Themes, Recurring Characters

Having taught Kingston over the years to legions of undergraduates, I know that the experience of reading her texts can be both exhilarating and confusing. Students almost always struggle initially to understand the plot of the texts, the relationship between characters and what motivates them, as well as the shifts between fact, fiction, and fantasy that so often characterizes Kingston's work. Once they have become accustomed to Kingston's elliptical writing style, they begin to appreciate how she questions almost all of the things that they had previously held to be irrefutable or factual: that there is a hard line between fiction and truth, that the history we learn in textbooks is a representative history of the nation, that the United States embraces its status as a nation of immigrants, and that race and gender have no impact on how one is treated or perceived in the United States. To put it simply, Kingston's work is all about breaking down the binaries that govern our lives and rule our interpretations of almost everything.

This goal of calling into question our assumptions about identity, history, nation, and genre manifests itself in multiple ways in Kingston's texts. Kingston's works are often labeled "postmodern" in their structures and approaches, because they "share with other postmodern pieces a tendency toward self-referentiality, a leaning toward pastiche and collage, quotation and parody, an eclectic embracing of all genres—both fictional and nonfictional, realistic and fantastic."[19] Indeed, the most notable aspect of Kingston's writing for those who are reading her for the first time is the way that her stories are put together. Kingston's works are often fractured in their construction—moving between narrators, genres, and across time—and her narratives often call attention to the gaps and inconsistencies within them. Another important and recurring characteristic in Kingston's texts is that her narrators never operate from a perspective of omniscience, and the texts often draw attention to this lack of knowledge and the extent to which they must imagine or fantasize events in order to make them comprehensible. Readers usually expect the stories that they read to be helmed by a narrator who has an authoritative relationship to the narrative that is being told; they also expect these stories to reflect an orderly understanding of cause and effect. *The Woman Warrior, China Men,* and Kingston's other works are filled with moments in which the narrator or protagonist concedes that he or she does not know the "truth" of a given matter and explores that lack of knowledge. Kingston's narrators do not speak from positions of authority and her texts very rarely offer any sense of closure to the reader. To offer just one example, in "No Name Woman," the first chapter of *The Woman Warrior,* the narrator confesses from the start that she has no way of knowing for certain who impregnated her paternal aunt or under what circumstances; instead, she imagines several scenarios in great detail, starting from what she deems the most likely (that her aunt was raped by some man in her village) to the least (that her aunt was a sexual free spirit). It is this self-reflexive emphasis on not-knowing that is one of Kingston's most consistent hallmarks and what is perhaps most identifiably postmodern about her work.

Kingston's texts also engage with language in a simultaneously playful and suspicious manner. In *The Woman Warrior,* the narrator notes that there is a word in Chinese for the female "I" that is also the word for slave; she rails, "Break the women with their own tongues!" The notion that language can be used to "break" a segment of the population, that its fundamental purpose is to oppress and exclude those who are powerless reflects Kingston's view that nothing can escape the dictates of power relations. Language does not reflect the truth of our world but rather works in the service of whatever ideology is in power. (I'll have more to say about the use of language in *The Woman Warrior* in chapter two.) Truth thus cannot be found in memory, history, or even experience—it cannot even be uncovered at the level of the sign (language) itself. This makes reading Kingston's works an incredibly challenging endeavor, as readers' questions regarding basic elements such as plot, character backgrounds, and so forth are never really answered and the narrative seems to take delight in the fact that nobody—not the narrator, not the author—can answer those questions. When Kingston talks in interviews about creating complexity and refusing to answer her reader's questions, this is exactly what she is referencing. Kingston would claim that she does not know any more than her readers what the "truth" of her narratives might be.

The power and perils of the linguistic sign is just one of the many issues that Kingston has explored and visited over the years. For the vast majority of her readers, she is best-known for writing about what it means to be Chinese in a deeply racist nation that has a strong history of anti-Chinese sentiment. Kingston is painfully aware of how her own family's history has been shaped by anti-Chinese exclusion and exploitation. With the passage of the Chinese Exclusion Act in 1882, the Chinese became the first national group in US history to be legally excluded from immigration. Laws passed on the state and federal level forbade the Chinese from testifying in court, owning property, marrying interracially, and living in certain parts of cities and towns. In the early twentieth century and extending into the mid-twentieth-century, Chinatowns were mostly "bachelor societies" with a huge imbalance of Chinese men to women. Chinese women were forbidden from entering the country due to the 1885 Page Act (which assumed that all Chinese or Mongolian women were prostitutes) and white American women risked losing their own citizenship status if they married a Chinese man. To make a living, Chinese men were forced into labor-intensive fields such as mining, railroad-building, restaurant work, and laundries. For Kingston, the experience of being Chinese in America is inextricable from the long history of anti-Chinese racism and exclusion that this country has practiced.[20] Kingston depicts the physical pain of her great-grandfather as he works the sugarcane fields; the anxiety of her grandfather as he attempts to purchase his American citizenship while working on the Transcontinental Railroad; the fear of her father as he attempts to stay ahead of the US government in order to avoid deportation back to a Communist China. These cares and worries are so pervasive that they are a part of her everyday life; even as a forty-plus-year-old woman, she worries in an interview that she will inadvertently get her father deported if she shares too many details of how he arrived in this country sixty years previously. The mistrust that Kingston and her family have for governmental institutions—both in the United States and in China—is reflected in her reluctance to go to China: she is afraid that the US government will deport her or her family for being Communist sympathizers or that the Chinese government will arrest her for aiding its capitalist enemies.[21]

The other major issue that Kingston explores consistently throughout her work is gender politics and the effects that sexism can have on individuals and communities. Kingston is widely known as a feminist author. She is indeed so strongly identified with women's experiences that several critics expressed surprise when *Tripmaster Monkey* was published and the protagonist was a man. Kingston's works constantly test the highly limited and limiting notion that a feminist can only write about or from the perspective of a woman. The feminism of a work like *The Woman Warrior* might be more "obvious" to a casual reader, but works like *China Men* and *Tripmaster Monkey* also embrace feminism in their attention to the social construction of gender and the oppressive effects a patriarchal system has on men of color as well as women. Kingston's critique of gender hierarchies is not just limited to acts of sexism—although examples of these abound in her works—but also investigates the ways that language and social practices construct women as less than human.

It is important to point out that Kingston's questioning of gender does not occur separately from her consideration of race and ethnicity; in fact, far from it. For Kingston, these issues are intimately and inextricably linked to each other. Her experiences as a racialized subject are tangled with her experiences as a woman; the racism she faces is inflected by her gender, and the sexism she decries is determined by the fact that she is Chinese. The sense of powerlessness that pervades her interactions with the racist "bosses" that she encounters in *The Woman Warrior* is as much a function of her gender as it is her race. In responding to their antiblack racism, the narrator emphasizes her high-pitched squeak of a voice that is easily dismissed by others. Kingston describes this voice in highly gendered terms—its hyperfemininity, unintentional as it is, is also what makes it ineffective and ignorable. The narrator's attempts to speak—to make her presence felt—"makes [her] throat bleed and takes up that day's courage."[22] Forcing oneself to speak when one is constantly rendered invisible or silent because of her gender or race requires a kind of physical and emotional effort that exhausts and shames. One is silenced and at the same time made to feel guilty about the silencing.

Literary Influences and Impact

Kingston's approach to literature has been informed by her experiences as a Chinese woman, as a peace activist, and as someone who came of age during the political and social tumult of the 1960s. She has been frank that she believes in the potential for literature to have a transformative effect on the attitudes and thinking of her readers. In talking about Wittman Ah Sing, the protagonist of her novel *Tripmaster Monkey,* Kingston has stated that she wanted his relationship to reading and the literary to be productive for himself and for the world. Wittman is an English graduate from Berkeley with a penchant for quoting Rainer Maria Rilke and Shakespeare. But Kingston didn't want him to "end up like Madame Bovary . . . or Don Quixote," two of literature's most romantic and self-destructive readers.[23] "Literature took [these character] to all the wrong places. I wanted to see whether Wittman can take all this wonderful literature and make the world a better place, given what he knows."[24] Kingston works toward this notion that literature can make the world a better place—utopian and idealistic as it sounds—in ways that are pedagogical; in other words, the way she talks about the role of literature is akin to the way we expect teachers to talk about how they impart knowledge and critical thinking skills to their students. Kingston imagines *active* readers who, when presented with something they don't understand or have never heard of, will scurry off to find out more about that subject: "I've had to come up with tricks, even changing the structure of a genre, to try to compensate for people's ignorance and encourage them to do research."[25] She assumes that her readers will engage with her texts as extensively as she does.

Kingston's approach toward writing has been influenced by an eclectic and unexpected mix of authors and texts. She has discussed the importance of Jade Snow Wong's *Fifth Chinese Daughter* (1950) to her emerging sense of herself as a Chinese girl growing up in the United States. Reading Wong for the first time as a sixth or seventh grader, Kingston notes that "For the first time I could see a person somewhat like myself in literature."[26] *Fifth Chinese Daughter* acted as an important corrective in Kingston's literary education, as most of the books she read as a child ignored or mocked Chinese characters. Kingston tells of reading the works of Louisa May Alcott (as many young girls and teenagers do), and "identifying with the March sisters" until the moment when she "came across this funny-looking little Chinaman. It popped out of the book. It pushed me into my place. I was him, I wasn't those March girls."[27] The realization that she wasn't and could never be the heroine of the novels she grew up loving spurred her desire to write about Chinese

Americans. Even if literary history wouldn't acknowledge the presence or importance of Chinese in the United States, Kingston wanted to assert her own American identity and right to live here as an American.

The influences of Chinese literature are not as explicit, although a Chinese man once told Kingston "how much *Tripmaster Monkey* reminded him of the *Dream of the Red Chamber*." This incident and others have cemented the somewhat vague notion within Kingston's mind that her writing has "roots in Chinese writing."[28] Kingston certainly invokes Chinese myths and histories in her writing frequently, whether it is the legend of Fa Mu Lan, the epic *Journey to the West,* or eighteenth-century Chinese novels—her writing is peppered with references to the Chinese tales her mother and other family members have told her. But it seems safe to say that Kingston's explicit literary influences have been from the world of Anglo-American letters. In fact, over the years, Kingston's discussion of literary influences repeatedly cites two texts that may surprise many readers: Virginia Woolf's *Orlando* (1928) and William Carlos Williams's *In the American Grain* (1925). According to Kingston, Woolf's *Orlando* sharpened her sense of herself as a feminist writer; Woolf also gave Kingston "permission" to "break through constraints of time, of gender, or culture."[29] Reading Woolf "made me free to write about people that are 150 years old and I don't have to be constrained by death or dates, and I can be free of being a man or a woman."[30]

In the American Grain is perhaps Kingston's favorite work; she has often expressed a wish that she had written it. For Kingston, Williams's incorporation of myth and legend into his ostensible history of the United States is "exactly the right way to write American history."[31] She makes an explicit link between Williams's work and her work, explaining that after "I finished [reading] *In the American Grain,* I thought there was going to be a part two because he ends the book with Abraham Lincoln. So I thought I would go ahead and read the rest of it; surely he must have written up to World War II. But it wasn't there. I just couldn't believe there wasn't a part two! My next thought was 'Part two is what I'm going to write.' I consider *China Men* as part two."[32] The choice seems an unusual one, and yet, based on what Kingston values as a writer and as a reader, her devotion to *In the American Grain* is not at all surprising. Kingston essentially states that she loves the book for what it leaves out as much as for what it contains. As Caroline Yang notes, "Williams' history spotlights figures and narratives that are rarely, if at all, seen together in the 'official' history of the Americas."[33] This kind of episodic construction of history—which emphasizes disjuncture—compels us to ask what or who is not included in traditional accounts of national history. It is precisely this notion of history as an evolving narrative, mixing genres and applying a poetic imagination and rhetoric in narrating events and personages in American history, that Williams captures in *In the American Grain* and that Kingston strives for in her own work.

While the list of Kingston's literary inspirations might be relatively short, there is no question that her impact on the writers who followed her—whether Asian American, feminist, memoirist, or postmodernist—has been strong. First and foremost, the publication of *The Woman Warrior* was a defining moment in what would become an Asian American literary renaissance. According to Sau-ling Wong, the commercial and critical success of *The Woman Warrior*

> has empowered and inspired subsequent generations of Chinese and other Asian American writers female and male, but especially female, to give voice to their experience. Kingston has raised the visibility of and expanded the readership for Asian American writers, and enhanced publishers' willingness to take risks and publish them. In particular, Kingston's pioneering work in matrilineal narratives featuring two or three generations of strong, inspiring female ancestors has generated numerous similar stories, of which Amy Tan's bestsellers *The Joy Luck Club* (1989) and *The Kitchen God's Wife* (1991) are particularly marketable and well known examples. . . . Whether or not these authors directly and consciously drew upon Kingston, and regardless of any other factor that might have affected publishing, it is undeniable that the market for matrilineal stories was greatly expanded by *The Woman Warrior*.[34]

In the years following the publication of *The Woman Warrior*, dozens of Asian American books (memoirs and novels) in which a conflicted mother-daughter relationship appears have been released: Joy Kogawa's *Obasan* (1981), Theresa Hak Kyung Cha's *Dictée* (1982), Ronyoung Kim's *Clay Walls* (1987), Amy Tan's *The Joy Luck Club* (1989), Jung Chang's *Wild Swans* (1991), Fae Ng's *Bone* (1993), Hisaye Yamamoto's "Seventeen Syllables" (1994), Wakako Yamauchi's "Songs My Mother Taught Me" (1994), Lisa See's *On Gold Mountain* (1995), Lan Cao's *Monkey Bridge* (1997), Nora Okja Keller's *Comfort Woman* (1998), Mira Stout's *One Thousand Chestnut Trees* (1998), Margaret Cho's stand-up film and book of the same name *I'm the One that I Want* (2000), Alice Wu's film *Saving Face* (2004), Lan Samantha Chang's *Inheritance* (2004), and Deanna Fei's *A Thread of Sky* (2010). Recently, a cluster of memoirs and essay collections have more humorously explored this emerging stereotype of the difficult, impossible-to-please Asian American mother: Annie Choi's *Happy Birthday or Whatever: Track Suits, Kimchee, and Other Family Disasters* (2007), Teresa and Serena Wu's *My Mom Is a Fob: Earnest Advice in Broken English from Your Asian American Mom* (2011), Amy Chua's *The Battle Hymn of the Tiger Mother* (2011), and Elaine Lui's *Listen to the Squawking Chicken: When*

Mother Knows Best, What's a Daughter To Do? (2013). It is safe to say, whether or not the authors were directly inspired by Kingston or not, *The Woman Warrior* paved the way for many of these books to be published and find readers.

As the above list indicates, Kingston's success has been hugely impactful in establishing for publishing houses the viability of Asian American literature and women's literature. This incredible achievement has also had a downside: Kingston's work has defined what the "Asian American experience" is not only to a generation of readers but also to a publishing industry eager to replicate the success of *The Woman Warrior* and *China Men*. For better or worse, the themes that Kingston wrote of in those two early works set up a notion of what Asian American literature should be that would be difficult for subsequent writers to shake. In the late 1980s, there were reports of publishing houses sending generic "Maxine Hong Kingston rejection slips" to aspiring Asian American authors and agents advising writers to read Kingston's work if they wished to be published.[35] Elizabeth Mehren, in a *Los Angeles Times* article on Gish Jen, speaks of Kingston's long shadow, calling Kingston the "literary godmother/grandmother" of other Asian American authors.[36] Some writers have less positive feelings about being compared to Kingston: Lan Samantha Chang, whose novella and short story collection *Hunger* was published to great acclaim in 2000, "cringe[d]" in a profile for the *New York Times* when she was called the "next Amy Tan or Maxine Hong Kingston."[37] Welcome or not, Kingston has cast a long shadow over a generation of Asian American women writers, who must not only deal with the difficulties of managing readers' expectations and stereotypes about what they should write about but also be prepared to be compared to Kingston, whether their work is similar to hers or not. Given the continuing popularity and relevance of Kingston's work, it seems likely that she will continue to exercise an outsized influence on the perception of Asian American literature. As Gish Jen notes admiringly, "We all have to write against her. . . . She's the person [who] defined in such a definitive way what the Chinese-American experience feels like. If you're going to try to redefine it, you're going to have to take on Maxine Hong Kingston."[38]

CHAPTER 2

The Woman Warrior
Memoirs of a Girlhood Among Ghosts

In 2013, Kingston was honored with the National Medal of Arts by President Barack Obama. The president noted in his speech for the occasion that "when I was first writing my first book [*Dreams from My Father,* 1995] and trying to teach myself how to write, *The Woman Warrior* was one of the books I read."[1] President Obama's remark that he looked to *The Woman Warrior* as a model for his own autobiographical endeavor indicates how influential Kingston's work has been to readers and writers of all kinds, transcending boundaries of race, gender, and class. It is a book that is beloved by readers, been written about extensively by critics and academics, and inspired a generation of writers from all walks of life to pen their own narratives of parental ambivalence, racial alienation, and gender formation. It has been the fountainhead for contemporary Asian American literature, helping to pave the way for the inclusion of Asian American issues in college classrooms and the institutionalization of Asian American Studies as an academic discipline. Its influence cannot be overstated.

That President Obama could cite *The Woman Warrior* as an inspiration nearly forty years after its initial publication also speaks to the phenomenal and enduring popularity the book has enjoyed.[2] Sau-ling Wong, in her introduction to *The Woman Warrior: A Casebook,* provides the numbers to back up these assessments. As late as 1989, *The Woman Warrior* was a perennial bestseller in trade paperback; as of 1996, nine hundred thousand hardcover and paperback copies had been sold, and as of 1997, the book had been translated into twenty languages. But it is not sales alone that have made *The Woman Warrior* a phenomenal success. It is a rare example of a book that has been a bestseller, a critical triumph, and a mainstay on syllabi in educational institutions across the country. Kingston is repeatedly credited as the most widely taught living American author, and *The Woman Warrior* as the most widely taught book by a living author on US college campuses, according to statistics compiled by the Modern Language Association, the professional organization for English and Foreign Language professors.[3] Poet Laureate Robert Haas has echoed this assessment of the book's pedagogical value, calling *The Woman Warrior* "*the* entry level book" for students adapting to university life (emphasis in original).[4] Laura Kang describes *The Woman Warrior* as one of the few "disciplinary brand names" in academia, putting Kingston in the company of figures such as Chaucer, Milton, and Shakespeare.[5] One final example of *The Woman Warrior*'s extraordinary popularity in the classroom: at the University of California at Berkeley, Kingston's alma mater and where she has long been a faculty member, *The Woman Warrior* was once taught in no fewer than twelve academic departments during the course of one academic year.[6]

Academia's interest in *The Woman Warrior* manifests itself in more ways than appearances on college syllabi. *The Woman Warrior* has generated a substantial body of secondary scholarship, as the subject of numerous articles, dissertations, and books.[7] A quick search of the MLA database reveals that *The Woman Warrior* has been the subject of 340 articles, books, and dissertations since its publication. David Li, for one, argues that academic critics have played an outsized role in securing the popularity of *The Woman Warrior* with the general reading public. These critics "maintain, transmit, and reproduce the meaning and significance of the book in academic institutions," and they "elevate the book to a status no Asian American text has hitherto enjoyed."[8] The constant presence of *The Woman Warrior* in college classrooms means that generations of American university students have read at least parts of the book, which means that they invest it with a level of intellectual and cultural capital that they then pass on to their peers and to succeeding generations. This along with the fact that *The Woman Warrior* is most likely the only Asian American text to which many readers will have any exposure means it carries a tremendous amount of weight for Asian American and non-Asian American readers alike.

The Woman Warrior consists of five interconnected chapters in which the narrator—an unnamed Chinese American woman—interweaves stories about her own childhood in Stockton's Chinatown with her mother's accounts of the lives of female family members and ancestors and her own versions of Chinese myths and legends. "No Name Woman," the first chapter in the volume, is the story of the narrator's paternal aunt. This aunt's name has been deliberately forgotten by the family, because she committed the crime of giving birth to a child who was not her husband's. Shunned by her village and cast out by her family, this No Name Aunt kills herself and her newborn by drowning in the family well. The next chapter, "White Tigers," consists of two parts. The first is the narrator fantasizing that she is the Chinese mythic heroine, Fa Mu Lan, the woman who took her father's place in battle, saved her village, and became a great general. In the second half of the chapter, the narrator contrasts this narrative of herself as a beloved and strong Chinese female leader with the reality of her "American life," in which racism, sexism, frustration, and a sense of inadequacy are inescapable. "Shaman" centers on the narrator's mother, Brave Orchid, the medical education she received in China before she came to the United States, and her struggles to raise her family in Stockton while working long hours at the laundry that she and her husband run. Brave Orchid's younger sister, Moon Orchid, is the focus of the fourth chapter, titled "At the Western Palace." This chapter is told from Brave Orchid's perspective, as she brings her more refined and timid younger sister to live in the United States and then coaxes and bullies Moon Orchid into confronting the husband who left her in China years ago for a new life in America. The shock of this encounter—and her husband's utter indifference to her upon being confronted with his abandonment—traumatizes Moon Orchid, leading her to lose her mind. In the final chapter, "A Song for Barbarian Reed Pipe," the Chinese American narrator from the first three chapters returns to describe her girlhood in Stockton: her confusion over her mother's behavior and the alienation and insecurities that she feels growing up Chinese in the United States. Despite the various traumas that the narrator and her family have endured and the confusion that she has felt over how to understand her Chinese American identity, *The Woman Warrior* closes on a hopeful note, with the story of Ts'ai Yen, a Chinese poet who was kidnapped by nomads and lived in exile for many years. Once she is returned to the Han, Ts'ai Yen writes a famous poem about her time with the nomads titled "Song for Barbarian Reed Pipe." The book ends with the famous and seemingly reassuring line: "It translated well."

This chapter examines some of the key themes in *The Woman Warrior,* as well as providing an analysis of the controversies that surrounded its publication, some of which still linger to this day. It begins by summarizing the staggering number of responses to the publication of *The Woman Warrior* from a wide range of readers. The chapter then addresses the critiques of some Chinese American readers of the book, focusing on those who were perturbed by the book's claim of autobiography and the way that such a genre designation might be interpreted by a largely white readership with a monolithic and highly exoticized vision of what it means to be Chinese or Chinese America. The genre controversy raises the question of whether or not ethnic and/or racially marked writers have some kind of responsibility to the communities with which they are identified: if these writers should attempt to correct the misapprehensions or racist narratives regarding their ethnic/racial group or if this assumption in and of itself represents a burden that is not expected of nonethnic writers. The rest of the chapter takes up some of the important motifs that appear throughout *The Woman Warrior* and explains how they contribute to the book's constructions of subjectivity, racial identity, gender, family, and nation.

Responses

How do we account for the popularity of this book, published by a then unknown, first-time author of Chinese descent? First of all, the book is compellingly and beautifully written. In its five connected chapters, Kingston movingly portrays what it means to grow up the daughter of Chinese parents in a Chinatown neighborhood that seems detached from the China of her family's past and the America of her own present. Moments of conjecture and narratives of fantasy follow without transition or comment passages that are grounded in the mundane life of a small child growing up in an ethnic enclave. The narrator's disjointed accounts of family tragedies are interspersed with sly moments of humor and sarcasm as well as interludes of poetic beauty and shocking violence. To give a brief example, at the start of "White Tigers," the narrator moves from describing the effects her mother's storytelling had on her childhood to an intricate daydream in which she herself is a young Fa Mu Lan. The fantasy sequence ends with the narrator's deadpan statement: "My American life has been such a disappointment" (45).

But aesthetic considerations alone do not make a book a bestseller. Rather it is a combination of factors—how it is marketed to a general audience, how it reflects the hopes or anxieties of its readership, or how it speaks to pressing contemporary social or political issues, to give a few examples—that can determine a book's success in terms of sales. Based on the response of readers, critics, and academics, it is clear that *The Woman Warrior* tapped into the zeitgeist of the 1970s and beyond. It was published at a time when feminism and ethnic solidarity were beginning to make themselves present not just in terms of the tastes of the American readership and the business of mainstream publishing but also in institutional ways, on college and university campuses in particular. Asian Americans like Kingston were becoming a more visible presence all across the country. A decade removed from the 1965 Hart-Celler Act, which had opened the door to large-scale immigration from Asia, and only a few years past the official end of American involvement in Vietnam and the start of a cautious détente between the United States and China, Americans were primed to be interested in reading about the experiences of Asian Americans.

Not only did *The Woman Warrior* depict the anguish, joy, and confusion embedded within the minority immigrant experience—a perennial and highly popular theme in American letters—it also focused on the particular perils of the mother-daughter relation at a time when second wave feminism was at the height of its influence. Many readers—feminist or not—strongly identified with Kingston's narrator struggle to find female role models within her rigidly patriarchal family. They found the description of the relationship between the narrator and the maternal figures in her life—particularly her very traditional Chinese mother—to be richly complex. This is not a text that depicts female empowerment as easy, charming, or even that much fun, and readers identified with that rawness and honesty. There are no idealized mothers, aunts, or sisters to cheer the narrator or each other on. The characters are deeply flawed and have often internalized to such a great extent the sexism that they have encountered that they don't recognize it as unusual or destructive. It is this messiness—the fact that Brave Orchid openly admonishes her daughter not to shame the family at the same time that she surreptitiously provides models for feminine resistance—to which female readers in particular have responded.

Its overwhelming commercial and critical success with readers of all races perhaps explains perhaps why *The Woman Warrior* has also been the most controversial of Kingston's works within the Asian American community. Some Asian American critics denounced it as pandering to white reading audiences, because they felt it presented a highly exoticized vision of Chinese culture and history as well as perpetuated negative stereotypes regarding Chinese and Chinese American men.[9] The rhetoric of these critiques has often been highly personal, labeling Kingston a sellout or race traitor. That the book has been championed by white feminists in particular seems particularly suspicious to some Chinese American critics: Jeffery Paul Chan sneered at Diane Johnson's review of *The Woman Warrior,* which appeared in the *New York Review of Books,* writing, "Never mind history, Johnson has uncovered a feminist."[10] Benjamin Tong called *The Woman Warrior* a "fashionably feminist work written with white acceptance in mind."[11] In these critics' minds, the fact that feminists had embraced the book only seemed to strengthen their opinion that the book was a pandering piece of propaganda written for a white readership eager to read about the victimization of women and the brutality of men in China. For these Asian American critics, the need by readers with feminist sympathies to have *The Woman Warrior* stand as *the* representative text of female struggle against patriarchy is an expression of a deep anti-Chinese racism, particularly against Chinese and Chinese American men. Reviews like Johnson's only reaffirmed to these critics that *The Woman Warrior* simply gratified the West's long-held racist beliefs regarding Chinese history, society, and gender relations.

While it is easy to dismiss these critics entirely because of their rigid ideas of ethnic identity and the deeply misogynistic language that lards their attacks, they nevertheless make a valid point regarding the racism that informs some feminist readings of the book. For example, David Li addresses the orientalist fantasy that undergirds Johnson's review of the book, calling particular attention to Johnson's claim that "Kingston reaches to the universal qualities of the female condition and female anger that the bland generalities of social science and that merely factual history cannot describe."[12] Li also rightly critiques Johnson's egregiously racist claim that "Chinese Americans are a notably unassimilated culture," a statement that is based on her belief that it "is not unusual in San Francisco to find fourth- or fifth-generation American-born Chinese who speak no English."[13] Similarly Sara Blackburn in her rave review calls *The Woman Warrior* a "psychic transcript of every woman I know—class, age, race, or ethnicity be damned," sweeping aside differences in race, class, and national origin.[14] Johnson and Blackburn's reviews reflect the extent to which *The Woman Warrior* was hailed a universal feminist text that spoke to or for all women, regardless of their ethnic or racial identification. In their hurry to identify with the narrator of *The Woman Warrior*—her sense of worthlessness at being a girl, her shame at her relative powerlessness against those who would oppress her, her isolation from both her American schoolmates and her Chinese family and neighbors—these critics engaged in the same kind of marginalizing and silencing acts as the ones that Kingston's narrator finds so oppressive. And as Li points out, this alignment of Chinese American women with universal female oppression also problematically positioned China and Chinese American men as the ultimate expression of patriarchy.

In one of the more nuanced contemporary critiques of *The Woman Warrior,* Katheryn Fong expresses the same concerns that the book feeds into already powerful narratives of Chinese patriarchy and sexism, but she takes a slightly different and much more constructive tack. While she admires Kingston's creativity and emotive language, she worries that "non-Chinese are reading your fiction as true accounts of Chinese and Chinese American history. That's the awesome price we Chinese Americans pay when so few of us—Jade Snow Wong, yourself, and a few others—are published. Your one experience, your one story, becomes the definitive description of all of us."[15] Fong's point that Kingston's "distortions" and "*very personal* description[s]" (emphasis in original) of Chinese and Chinese American history and experience will be read as "fact" by most readers, and that her words will come to "represent the identity of all Chinese American women" informs her discomfort with reading the book.[16] Critic King-Kok Cheung argues that the antipathy of Chinese American readers like Fong stems from the knowledge that white readers tend to approach ethnic memoirs "as pure ethnography, rather than as self-conscious narratives that answer to provocative silences."[17] It is this ethnographic impulse among readers that "has sparked protracted debate among Asian American critics concerning 'authenticity.'"[18] The concern is that writers like Kingston unwittingly end up reinforcing certain powerful stereotypes regarding the Chinese, which reinforces the notion within a reader that he or she can "know" China or Chinese America after reading the book. Indeed, in reading over some of the contemporary reviews of *The Woman Warrior,* it is clear that Fong's anxieties were well placed. As Fong feared, some readers focused particular attention on the work as an "authentic" rendering of China; these readers considered *The Woman Warrior* to be an authoritative source on Chinese women and the Chinese American experience. In a multitude of interviews that Kingston has granted over the years, the nature of the interviewers' questions—essentially asking Kingston to authenticate what the book depicts—attests to the fact that many readers view the text as ethnographic. Many of the book's reviewers also seem to feel authorized to make sweeping statements about China and the Chinese American community with which the narrator struggles so mightily.

Kingston addresses both the racism of her white readership and the antagonism of her Chinese American critics in an essay titled "Cultural Mis-readings by American Reviewers," which came out after the publication of *The Woman Warrior.* Kingston sharply responds to Chinese American critics who felt that the book itself portrayed China and the Chinese American experience through an orientalist lens. Kingston resents those who critique her because they believe that her experiences will inevitably be construed as representative of *all* Chinese Americans. She argues that these kinds of concerns rob the Chinese American or ethnic American artist the freedom to define him or herself outside of racist and sexist norms: "Why must I 'represent' anyone besides myself? Why should I be denied an individual artistic vision? And I do not think I wrote a 'negative' book, as the Chinese American reviewer said; but suppose I had? Suppose I had been so wonderfully talented that I wrote a tragedy? Are we Chinese Americans to deny ourselves tragedy?"[19] Kingston argues that the logic of her Chinese American critics severely limits what future Chinese or Asian American authors can write about. Stories that depict violence, injustice, or calamity within the Chinese American community would be off-limits to authors because they may reinforce racist stereotypes held by readers. For Kingston, these critiques have only intensified the burden of representation that Chinese American authors must unfairly bear; it is these critics, in her eyes, who are pandering to white readership by attempting to sanitize the realities of Chinese and Chinese American history and experience.

The bulk of the essay, however, is reserved for Kingston's blistering response to the essentializing and exoticizing work of her Caucasian reviewers. These misreadings are as present in the book's many glowing reviews as they are in the reviews that panned the book. She humorously but pointedly blasts reviewers who write that *The Woman Warrior* captures the "inscrutable," "foreign," "oriental" "mysterious," and "exotic" nature of China.[20] Just as bad are the reviewers who seem to think that Kingston is a Chinese national (rather than Chinese American); one reviewer named Kate Herigges writing for the *Boston Phoenix* states that the book and its author are "ineffably Chinese."[21] The lede in another newspaper review explains that Kingston "is a Chinese woman, even though her place of birth was Stockton, California."[22] As Kingston herself points out, such a statement is completely nonsensical, but here we have incontrovertible proof that for many Americans, the Chinese simply cannot be American, even when they were born, raised, and have lived in the United States their entire lives as American citizens, as Kingston has.[23] Kingston writes that the most upsetting review was from Michael T. Malloy in the *National Observer* who objected that the book *wasn't exotic enough:* when he picked up the book, he was eagerly expecting a foray into mysterious China but instead was confronted with an entirely mundane and unexotic example of "mainstream . . . American feminist literature."[24] In dedicating an entire essay to the egregiously racist ways that her work has been read, Kingston is clearly exasperated and disheartened: "I find it sad and slow that I have to *explain* [why the reviews are so offensive]. Again. If I use my limited time and words to explain, I will never get off the ground. I will never get to fly."[25] Kingston alludes to the fact that even for a successfully published and critically acclaimed author, the casual racism and sexism of readers and reviewers can be burdensome, forcing her to take time away from her creative endeavors in order to explain herself or her text.

As these comments indicate, *The Woman Warrior* has drawn more than its fair share of racist and sexist comments. But it has also sparked tremendous dialogue about the complex construction and constitution of Chinese American community and identity. Supporters of Kingston have responded that the book represents a "multivalent" approach to Chinese American literary history that seeks to construct a Chinese American female identity that resists racism and sexism's power to silence women *and* men.[26] Cheung argues that Kingston "emphatically resists the opposition of fact and imagination in the face of received falsehood and historical silence."[27] In other words, Kingston does not try to counter pervasive racist notions about the Chinese by claiming that her own narratives are more authentic. It is clear that with the passing of time, *The Woman Warrior* has outlasted its orientalizing reviewers and emerged triumphant from the "Chinese American pen wars," as many of the arguments of her Chinese American male critics seem now to be archaic and misguided, steeped in the language of misogyny and racial essentialism. It also seems certain that the book's ability to provoke discussion, debate, and even hostility is why it continues to fascinate and engage readers forty years after its initial publication. The debate surrounding *The Woman Warrior* did more than just highlight Kingston's ability to challenge conventions and provoke discussion; it helped to ensure Kingston's place in the American literary canon. The book also had an impact far beyond Kingston herself: its success paved the way for the emergence of a whole raft of Asian American authors, from Amy Tan to Amy Chua, and its complex approach to questions of gender and race has heavily influenced the critical conversation in a number of academic disciplines like Asian American studies and gender studies.

Genre: Is It or Isn't It?

In a letter to critic Shawn Wong dated November 3, 1976, Kingston noted with delight that bookstores had been shelving *The Woman Warrior* in a variety of spots: "I've seen it under fiction, non-fiction, sociology, anthropology, biography, woman's lit, Chinese, Asian, general. This confusion really makes me feel good."[28] Kingston's glee that her book has caused no small amount of "confusion" is a characteristic response for an author who has repeatedly expressed pride in the fact that readers find her works difficult. In an interview with Karen Horton in 1979, Kingston stated "I try to be convoluted" and expressed no desire to publish "popular stories" marked by an "accessible" writing style.[29]

The inability of bookstore managers to easily categorize *The Woman Warrior* proved to be just the appetizer in a multicourse feast regarding the book's genre; if the initial confusion delighted Kingston then the ensuing decades of critical wrangling must have enraptured her. The debate has often revolved around whether or not *The Woman Warrior* can or should be called nonfiction. The problem with this conversation is that, for the most part, there is very little critical questioning of the categories of "fiction" or "nonfiction." The Asian American critics who castigated *The Woman Warrior* tended to do so because they felt the book was inauthentic in its representation of Chinese American culture, whereas some of the book's most ardent admirers thought it offered an unfiltered look into the mysterious world that Chinatowns represent. Despite their seeming opposition, both camps uncritically rely upon the distinction between fiction and nonfiction and the notion that narratives of ethnic experience can (or should) be clearly and easily marked as one or the other.

Given how contentious and confusing the issue of genre has been over the years, it might be useful here to set down a chronology, pieced together from various interviews and articles, regarding how *The Woman Warrior* came to be categorized as nonfiction and Kingston's responses to that categorization. Kingston has consistently articulated one notion through the years to explain the book's genre classification: that publishers felt that reading audiences would find a nonfiction version of a Chinese American woman's life more appealing or readily understandable than a fictional account.[30] Kingston's agent sent a partial manuscript to publishing houses Norton and Little Brown, but both rejected the project because, according to Kingston, they didn't understand what the book was. Ultimately, editors at Knopf, although unsure of how to market the book from the start, decided to classify *The Woman Warrior* as nonfiction because, as Kingston noted, nonfiction was thought to be an easier "sell" to reading audiences. While Kingston says that her initial preference was not to saddle the book with a label of fiction or nonfiction, Knopf insisted to her "You have to categorize" the book.[31] Kingston states, in an interview with Mandelbaum, that Knopf thought the book was more marketable as nonfiction because "publishers think American readers have no imagination. Also, it's easier to get on talk shows when it's nonfiction. Television producers want a writer up there embodying everything that's in the book."[32] This idea that the writer "embody" the book is particularly relevant for writers of color, who are expected to speak for the experiences of their ethnic community.

As with any origin story, slightly different accounts exist. Over the years and over the course of a dozen interviews, Kingston has expressed contradictory thoughts regarding the genre of *The Woman Warrior* and *China Men*. In an early interview with Gary Kubota for the *Hawai'i Observer,* Kingston states that "I thought of [*The Woman Warrior*] as a novel when I mailed it out to the publishers. I felt it had to be defined in that form because of the fictional techniques I used in the story. . . . I might have felt the same emotions as the main character, the girl, at moments in my life."[33] In this interview, Kingston articulates a distinction between form and content that she would return to throughout the years as a way of differentiating nonfiction from fiction: that the content of *The Woman Warrior* and *China Men* reflected events in her or her family's lives, but that the manner in which she conveyed their narratives transformed those memories into fiction. In the above instance, Kingston's version of the book's publication portrays herself as a relatively passive bystander in the discussions on how to categorize *The Woman Warrior.* The decision on genre—as well as the decision regarding the title—was made by editors and agents, not by Kingston. Kingston's explanation that marketing was a determining factor in the book's genre classification dovetails with what Charles Elliot, Kingston's editor at Knopf, is reported to have said about the publication process of *The Woman Warrior:* "Well, first novels are hard to sell. I knew [*The*

Woman Warrior] would stand a stronger chance of selling well as nonfiction autobiography. It could have been called anything else."[34] As David Li notes, "Literary classification is equivalent to the packaging of a final product, which is not always determined by the producer or author."[35] Elliot's point suggests that the reading public approaches autobiographies differently than they do novels; indeed, many critics have noted that the success of the ethnic autobiography as a genre in the United States stems from the fact that readers look to these works to reveal some kind of truth (often exoticizing or titillating) about the ethnic community it purports to represent. Li notes that this compulsion to align ethnic experience with autobiographical genres has "the effect of depriving Asian American expression of its credibility as an imaginative art and reducing it to some subliterary status, serving the role of social scientific data, an encompassing reflection of Asian American totality."[36] In other words, people want to read Asian American works when they think it will offer an "authentic" glimpse into Asian American life.

In subsequent years, Kingston's stance on the issue has changed. In a 1987 interview with Paula Rabinowitz, Kingston suggested that the decision to publish *The Woman Warrior* as nonfiction was at least partly her own. Her ambivalence on the subject of genre manifests itself when she notes, "Sure, I could have classified them [*The Woman Warrior* and *China Men*] as fiction," an admission that suggests that had she wanted, she could have overturned the publisher's decision to publish the books as nonfiction. In 1986, Kingston told Kay Bonetti that *The Women Warrior* and *China Men* are a "new kind of biography. . . . I tell the imaginative lives and the dreams and the fictions of real people."[37] This is a thought that she would repeat over the years: that because her books portray the fantasies and/or imagined lives of "real" people they straddle the categories of fiction and nonfiction, emerging as a hybridized version of both. In another interview, Kingston explains that the relationship between fiction and nonfiction "doesn't bother me very much. It bothers other people more."[38] Kingston's ever shifting attitudes on the line between fiction and nonfiction is an indicator of how difficult it is to pin down the line between the genres, and how much of that distinction depends upon a variety of factors—audience, marketing, readers' perceptions, authors' perceptions—rather than some kind of easy identifiable definition.

At times, however, Kingston's way of talking about *The Woman Warrior* strongly suggests that it is a rather straightforward autobiography. While we as literary scholars should not always take what an author says about his or her work as the final word, it is certainly noteworthy that Kingston talks about *The Woman Warrior* and *China Men* in a way one might expect a person to talk about his or her autobiography. Interviewers repeatedly ask her to elaborate on events described in *The Woman Warrior,* assuming that these events really happened as described and that Kingston experienced them. Kingston almost always willingly complies and never corrects interviewers by pointing out that fiction and fact are blurred in her works. For example, in response to a question from an interviewer regarding the speechlessness of the narrator as a young child in *The Woman Warrior* ("Did [you] really go through a period in which [you] just didn't speak to anyone?"), Kingston's response is in the affirmative.[39] Kay Bonetti in another interview inquires of Kingston: "When you drew your silence in the first three years of school and could not speak, out of shyness and fear and not knowing English, you drew these wonderful pictures and then covered them all in black paint."[40] Kingston explains what the black paint meant to her—she saw them as curtains covering the picture she had drawn—unproblematically equating her own experience to the narrator of the book. She contributes to the confusion by seemingly authenticating certain parts of her family's story as narrated in *The Woman Warrior,* noting for example that the story of her No Name Aunt has been verified by her father and that her descriptions of her family's village in China are accurate:[41] "The fear was that when I got there I would see something so different that it would invalidate everything I had written. But I went to my parents' village. I went to the rooms that are described in 'No Name Woman.' I saw the well where she drowned. And I felt really good because I found that the China I had imagined is very much like the China that's there. The trip gave me a lot of faith in the power of my imagination."[42]

At other times, Kingston strives to distinguish what she has written from her own life. She points out in an interview with Paul Skenazy that the narrator in *The Woman Warrior* has no name: "Her name isn't Maxine; that's my name. I see this as a literary text that's very separate from myself. Throughout [the text], nobody calls her anything."[43] In a 1991 interview with Shelley Fisher Fishkin, Kingston elaborates that when readers question whether or not *The Woman Warrior* is "real," she feels that they are having the response she means them to have: "People give me back the questions I give them. . . . You know, I can answer these questions but then that means I just answer it for me."[44] The implication? The reader must answer questions about genre for him or herself.

Kingston's range of responses to the question of whether or not the events in *The Woman Warrior* "really" happened suggests, according to Patricia Chu, that neither her Chinese past nor her American present can "adequately acknowledge her diasporan culture or the particularities of her position as a Chinese American."[45] In other words, the Manichean distinctions that are made between genres of writing or the binaristic nature of racialized identity (e.g., "America: love it or leave it") cannot easily explain or capture the kinds of experiences and histories that Kingston and other Chinese Americans—past or present—have lived through. Given how much of Chinese American history was never recorded or has otherwise been deemed unworthy of remembrance, questioning genres of fact and fantasy and creating narratives that intermingle the two easily (as Kingston does) seems a particular condition of the Chinese American experience that cannot be avoided.

Furthermore, Kingston's ambivalence about genre and *The Woman Warrior* and her nuanced and sometimes contradictory approaches to the question fit in with trends in autobiography studies of the past several decades. The traditional reading of autobiography is that it "represents the achievement of metaphysical selfhood."[46] Feminist critics have pointed out that such a definition of the genre can only reflect the lives of the most privileged subjects, that is, white males. Katherine Lee argues that "rather than view autobiography as a narrative through which the self springs fully formed, feminist theorists have defined the genre as one that encompasses negotiation and contradiction, in which the self, by dint of its ties to social forces, cannot (and does not necessarily desire to) achieve transcendence."[47] Lee points out how often the language of transcendence still informs much of what is written about *The Woman Warrior* even as the narrative resists any kind of transcendent resolution. Kingston begins *The Woman Warrior* asking, "What is Chinese tradition and what is the movies?" (5–6) and concludes it with the hardly definitive statement, "I continue to sort out what's my childhood, just my imagination, just my family, just the village, just movies, just living" (205). These statements and questions underline Min Song's argument that the "focal point of *The Woman Warrior* is the narrator's lack of knowledge."[48] This lack of knowledge on the part of the narrator might seem completely contradictory, given the fact that we expect the subject of memoir to have an understanding of his or her own life. But Kingston's refusal to position herself as the font of knowledge dovetails with what Linda Hutcheon has called the genre of postmodern autobiography, into which category Hutcheon places *The Woman Warrior* along with memoirs by Christa Wolf, Michael Ondaatje, and Roland Barthes. According to Hutcheon, these new kinds of autobiographies "not only challenge what we consider to be literature (or rather, Literature) but also what was once assumed to be the seamless, unified narrative representations of subjectivity in life writing."[49] Feminist rethinking about the constitution of subjectivity and its relationship to text have influenced these postmodern autobiographies.[50] But the link between feminism and autobiography as a genre is not one without tension. King-Kok Cheung summarizes the tension between feminist and ethnic studies scholars grappling with the question of autobiography and the minoritized subject: "Feminist scholars of autobiography have suggested that women writers often shy away from 'objective' autobiography and prefer to use the form to reflect a private world, a subjective vision, and the life of the imagination. *The Woman Warrior* . . . is quite in line with such an autobiographical tradition. Yet for a 'minority' author to exercise such artistic freedom is perilous business because white critics and reviewers persist in seeing creative expressions by her as no more than cultural history."[51]

The book's ambiguous adherence to the "rules" of genre seems to make twenty-first century readers simultaneously more and less comfortable. Jess Row, in a highly laudatory piece for *Slate* magazine on the thirtieth anniversary of *The Woman Warrior*'s publication, encapsulates the contradictory responses that readers have to the notion that the lines between nonfiction and fiction might be blurred or a matter of perspective. On the one hand, Row cites *The Woman Warrior* as a "book without a genre. At various times, it has been described as a memoir, an autobiography, a novel, a manifesto; yet anyone who spends 10 minutes with it understands that none of these labels really apply." So far so good. And yet in the next sentence, Row reveals a sense of anxiety regarding *The Woman Warrior*'s manipulation of generic conventions. Row writes that there is a difference between how Kingston writes about her life and someone like James Frey, that distinction being that Kingston, unlike Frey, "deliberately acknowledges that to write autobiography is to stand at the borderline between memory and invention."[52] Row's invocation of James Frey and his widely discredited memoir *A Million Little Pieces* (2003) is an interesting one and reflects the extent to which American publishing and readers have changed and hardened their attitude toward genre since the mid-1970s. In an atmosphere in which readers have become increasingly suspicious of writers as they fabricate important details of their lives (like Frey in *A Million Little Pieces*) or even invent entirely new personas, lives, and histories (like Binjamin Wilkomirski in *Fragments* [1995]), the fantastical elements of Kingston's own work of nonfiction must be justified. The *Slate* article highlights how her work—which is highly lionized and canonized—must be differentiated from the "frauds" like Frey and Wilkomirski.

Talk Story and Identity

The Woman Warrior famously opens with these words: "You must not tell anyone what I am about to tell you" (1). The speaker of this warning—the narrator's mother, Brave Orchid—then proceeds to tell her daughter the story of the narrator's disgraced paternal aunt, who killed herself after the village discovered that she had given birth to a baby while her husband was on Gold Mountain. It begins, in other words, with an act of unspeakable oppression and an act of quiet defiance. The mother's words to her adolescent daughter can be understood in two ways: as a warning whose purpose is to cow the narrator into behaving according to strict gender codes of the Chinese and Chinese American communities and as a rebellion against those very codes since they require silence on the part of the community in order to exact their power. What becomes clear to the narrator is that these two interpretations are not mutually exclusive—in other words, her mother means to frighten her into conformity, but she also offers her a model and a means to disobey through speech. Brave Orchid resists the very gendered and familial structures that she seems to be perpetuating. For Jeanne Smith, it is this contradictory quality that makes Brave Orchid—"whose very name is a paradox"—a trickster "who undermines and upsets the injunctions that she delivers" and who passes on this trickster legacy to her daughter. This legacy is "necessarily complex because [Brave Orchid] represents for her daughter the oppressive authority of Chinese culture, especially regarding acceptable female behavior. Yet through her actions and her stories, Brave Orchid sends vivid messages that subvert her authoritarian proclamations."[53] In passing down the story to her daughter—even as a cautionary tale—Brave Orchid insures that the aunt though nameless will not be forgotten

As this initial passage hints, narration (or as Kingston calls it "talking story") is a crucial act and trope throughout the book. So central is the notion of talking to *The Woman Warrior* that David Leiwei Li calls the structure of book a "Chinese box of 'talk stories,' through which Kingston conceives and perceives herself."[54] Kingston describes "talk story" as an oral tradition, one that blurs the lines between the historical and the imaginary, the national and the domestic, reality and fantasy. With talk story as the organizing principle of *The Woman Warrior,* it becomes clear why the uncertainty about genre persists; "talk story" as practiced within the Hong family is premised on the notion that narratives reflect and combine an oral ("talk") and historical ("story") component in order to convey meaning. This initial passage also indicates the highly ambivalent role that speech or voice plays in this text. However, the tendency amongst readers and critics is to emphasize the ways speech becomes a form of resistance or liberation. In analyzing *The Woman Warrior,* critics tend to link acts of speech within the book to moments of self-invention, knowledge, and freedom. Linda Morante, in her article "Silence to Song: The Triumph of Maxine Hong Kingston," exemplifies this critical stance that words equal empowerment while silence equals death: "In *The Woman Warrior,* Kingston inextricably knots this pursuit of words with the process of self-creation and survival. Silence obliterates identity" while "articulation creates selfhood."[55] The critical valorization of voice follows a long Western philosophical history that speech is a sign that a subject has reached a political consciousness; in contemporary politics, we often construct voice as a form of resistance against injustice. Voice, in other words, becomes a metaphor for political power.

Certainly there are many examples within *The Woman Warrior* of speech as an act of defiance against racist or patriarchal hierarchies. Brave Orchid's decision to tell the story of the disgraced aunt, her sharing of the myth of Fa Mu Lan, and her long narratives related to the family's history—triumphant and tragic—become a source of meaning as well as confusion for her daughter. As readers, we tend to notice most the ways in which *The Woman Warrior* at times equates speech with personal or political empowerment. Injunctions against speech are a central trope throughout *The Woman Warrior,* but it is particularly the first chapter, "No Name Woman," that grapples with the consequences of the enforced silences with which the text concerns itself. Her mother repeatedly forbids the narrator that she knows the story of his sister: "Don't let your father know that I told you" (5) and "Your father does not want to hear her name" (15). The narrator grew up believing that "sex was unspeakable and words so strong and father so frail that 'aunt' would do my father mysterious harm" (15–16). While Brave Orchid's cautionary tale about the No Name Woman offers a terrifying version of talk story (do not tell; do not shame), it also reflects the power that words are accorded within this family; the mere mention of this woman's name or the word "sex" will somehow destroy her father. The narrator believes that her words have the power to hurt and maim those who are ostensibly more powerful than she.

The conclusion of *The Woman Warrior* also exemplifies this notion that speech or speaking out can be empowering. Brave Orchid tells the narrator the story of Ts'ai Yen, the female poet who is kidnapped and raises a family in exile. Her children grow up laughing at the sound of their mother's native tongue. It is only when she writes poems about her life and family in China that her children and the rest of the barbarians finally understand her "sadness and anger" (209). When she is ransomed and returned to her father's people, she brings "her songs back from the savage lands, and one of the three that has been passed down to us is 'Eighteen Stanzas for a Barbarian Reed Pipe,' a song that the Chinese sing to their own instruments. It translated well" (209). This final sentence has been a recurring trope in critical discussions of Kingston's work, and although it is not cited as frequently within mainstream articles, it symbolizes the critical narrative of unambiguous empowerment that many want to read into *The Woman Warrior.* Kingston herself found the figure of the exiled poet to be a much more compelling one than Fa Mu Lan, and she has spoken of how she wished the message of peace embedded within Ts'ai Yen's story was acknowledged in the book's title, which instead focuses on martial achievement and war.

Perhaps the best-known example within the text of the transformative powers of envoicement is in the chapter "White Tigers." At the start of the chapter, the narrator explains that she "at last" understood that she had grown up with "a great power, my mother talking-story." The use of "at last" is temporally misplaced; since this is the start of the chapter, we would expect to read "at first." The famous passage follows: "After I grew up, I heard the chant of Fa Mu Lan, the girl who took her father's place in battle. Instantly I remembered that as a child I had followed my mother about the house, the two of us singing about how Fa Mu Lan fought gloriously and returned alive from war to settle in the village. I had forgotten this chant that was once mine, given to me by my mother, who may not have known its power to remind. She said I would grow up a wife and a slave, but she taught the song of the warrior woman, Fa Mu Lan. I would have to grow up a warrior woman" (19–20). This is a moment of pure female communion with the chant of Fa Mu Lan connecting mother and her daughter together across generations and time. The narrator emphasizes that this is a story that is meant to be spoken or sung; it is not passed down in books or in writing but accrues its significance precisely because it is oral. The chant is also a gift from Brave Orchid to the narrator, a talisman to protect her from the worst that sexism or racism can do. The power of talk story stems from the fact that it gives those who are disempowered or marginalized the ability to resist forces that seem otherwise superior and overwhelming. This is of particular importance to the narrator as she attempts to navigate the sexism that she faces as a young woman within her Chinese American "village" and family *and* the racism (tinged with heavy doses of sexism) that she confronts as a Chinese American woman outside of Chinatown.

To me, this passage has always had a valedictory ring, as if it belongs at the *end* of the narrative rather than its start. It is telling that one of the most passages most associated with the trope of speech-as-power occurs near the start of the narrative—the fact that the narrator's epiphany, prefaced with "at last," is actually situated at first reflects the extent to which Kingston disrupts our expectations regarding narrative and progress. Any knowledge that the narrator gleans, any resolution that she reaches for the conflicts in her life—these are but temporary milestones that may be undone or prove to be illusory. Remembering the chant of Fa Mu Lan feels like a moment of empowerment until one realizes that at the end of the chapter, the narrator describes her relationship to "her people" as effectively one of exile.

I would argue that there are many more instances in *The Woman Warrior* where voice—speaking up, talking back, making one's presence felt—acts in a harmful or detrimental way. In fact, I would go so far as to say that there are many overlooked moments within *The Woman Warrior* where silence is portrayed as not just expedient but also powerful and empowering. Despite readers' and scholars' efforts to read *The Woman Warrior* as a progress narrative in which the narrator's ability to speak of the racism and sexism that troubles her is a sign that she has achieved a harmonious understanding of herself as a raced and gendered subject, the book actually presents a picture of identity formation in which silence *and* speech are equally constitutive. Erin Ninh argues that when it comes to this book, there is a critical tendency to "tone down" or "explain away" contradictions and fissures that resist closure.[56] Moments, language, images, sections that speak to ambivalence, stuck-ness, regression, and circularity are simply ignored. Similarly, the moments in which voice or silence are represented ambivalently tend to be ignored. In point of fact, *The Woman Warrior* interrogates the notion that the most politically viable way of establishing one's subjectivity is by finding one's "voice"; it questions any kind of sweeping equation of voice with power or voicelessness with powerlessness.

The story of the No Name Aunt is a perfect example of how speech can both be a sign of resistance as well as a form of oppression. As the narrator states, the story of the aunt encapsulates the notion that "words [are] so strong" that they can harm the patriarch of the household that seems particularly empowering. And the narrator's claim that the silence of the family and community regarding the aunt is a form of "punishment" emphasizes the power of the word. But what tends to be ignored is the fact that in speaking (or in this case, writing), the narrator is not entirely certain that her aunt approves of what she is doing: "My aunt haunts me—her ghost drawn to me because now, after fifty years of neglect, I alone devote pages of paper to her, though not origamied into houses and clothes. I do not think she always means me well. I am telling on her, and she was a spite suicide, drowning herself in the drinking water. The Chinese are always very frightened of the drowned one, whose weeping ghost, wet hair hanging and skin bloated, waits silently by the water to pull down a substitute" (16). The image of the aunt—the "spite" suicide"—haunting her niece for "telling on her" suggests that not all speech acts are redemptive and empowering, even when they are done to right a past injustice. The narrator specifically says that she is "telling on" the aunt, a choice of verb that suggests that in speaking, the narrator is harming the aunt, that her talking-story on this matter is tantamount to a betrayal. The narrator's fear that she is betraying the aunt as much as she is resisting her family's imposed silence reminds the reader that there is no easy solution to a past oppression—that restitution cannot be granted simply by speaking of the wrongs of the past.

The narrator's ambivalent notion that words complicate rather than resolve past injustices and silences is echoed in the ways that she feels that they are weaponized against her by her family. Throughout "White Tigers," the narrator is crippled by the kinds of comments she hears growing up from her family members and other inhabitants of Chinatown. The narrative promotes the sense that language is patriarchal and misogynistic in its construction; it cannot therefore be used unproblematically in the resistance of Chinese American women. When the neighbors quote a string of derogatory comments about girls as proof that the narrator is worthless and a burden to her family—"Feeding girls is like feeding cowbirds," "There's no profit in raising girls. Better to raise geese than girls," or "When you raise girls, you're raising children for strangers" —her response is to thrash about the floor while screaming "I'm not a bad girl" over and over again, which the narrator later realizes is tantamount to screaming "I'm not a girl" (46). The very notion of "badness" here is inscribed into the word "girl" itself—to call someone a bad girl is redundant as being a girl is simply bad enough. This point is reiterated when the narrator notes that there "is a "Chinese word for the female *I*—which is 'slave.' Break the women with their own tongues" (47). The abuse that women suffer is not just inflicted upon them by others—it is something that they must inflict upon themselves in the course of speaking. Speech in this case isn't affirming and talking back isn't terribly effective. The manifold and convoluted ways that language works is evidenced in the narrator's feelings toward her own parents. She writes that "from afar, I can believe my family loves me fundamentally" (52). But her memory of hearing her parents say horribly sexist things "because that is what one says about daughters" haunts her. There is no easy cultural translation of this kind of misogyny, no easy way to reconcile what she is hearing her mother and father say and the love (she hopes) they feel for her as their child.

Perhaps the most famous scene in the book is one in which the narrator attacks and vilifies another Chinese American girl, one who is even more silent than the narrator herself. Amongst other things, the narrator accuses her classmate of being "a plant. Do you know that? That's all you are if you don't talk. If you don't talk, you can't have a personality. You'll have no personality and no hair. You've got to let people know you have a personality and a brain" (180). This is the book's starkest and most disturbing articulation of the equation between talk and presence. Intelligence, beauty, "personality"—all of these qualities must be proven by the ability to "talk" regardless of whether or not one has anything to say. This scene is an extended monologue of the narrator verbally (and sometimes physically) assaulting her noncompliant and entirely silent opponent—she is the one speaking, "talking" and perpetrating violence. The narrator tells the silent girl "I'm doing this for your own good," a common excuse for abusive behavior, and in this case implying that the violence and trauma inflicted upon the victim comes from a place of love and caring. The narrator admonishes her victim, "Don't you dare tell anyone I've been bad to you. Talk.

Please talk" (181). There are two contradictory orders being given here: "Don't you dare tell" and "Talk." As many have noted, the narrator hates this Chinese American classmate, because she is a stand-in for the narrator's own sense of voicelessness and powerlessness within a racist and sexist society. But the assumption that speech equals subject, a correlation that the narrator has clearly picked up on from what she witnesses and experience around her, leads in this case to an act of violence. The narrator uses the idea of voice to silence those who don't conform to the gender conventions that she espouses. This is not to say that the narrator's victim is entirely silent: she weeps and moans throughout the episode with rivers of snot and tears streaming down her face, much to the narrator's disgust. Although she is silent throughout this scene, her body nevertheless "speaks" eloquently and extensively of her suffering. But because Kingston believes so completely in the notion that speech equals presence and that equals power, she cannot pay attention to the nonverbal cues that the little girl shares.

The narrator's experiences with words suggests that language is always fraught with gender and racial conventions that are difficult—if not impossible—to escape. These examples highlight the importance of language in the narrator's sense of her worthlessness. Language itself betrays the narrator—she cannot use it to combat the injustices to which she is subject. While language is extremely adept at excluding, marginalizing, and deflating, it is extremely ineffective, Kingston suggests, in fighting those kinds of moves. To cite one example, in describing her sister's experience with public speaking as a child, Kingston emphasizes how the girl's voice sounds as if she is "weeping and [being] strangl[ed]" at the same time. The narrator's own voice she calls a "crippled animal running on broke legs"; even though her voice can be loud, it sounds as if it is full of "splinters . . . bones rubbing ragged against one another" (168–69). As an adult, Kingston always protests the casual racism she encounters in the men—"business-suited in their modern American executive guise, each . . . two feet taller than I am and impossible to meet eye to eye" (48)—for whom she works; and yet her principled protests against their comments and business practices do absolutely nothing to alter their beliefs. "I don't like that word" she squeaks to a boss at an art-supply store who uses the word "nigger." He does not even deign to respond to her objection. Another boss simply fires her when she objects to an industry banquet being held at a restaurant that is being picketed by CORE and the NAACP; her voice in that case is "whispered" and "unreliable" (49). These are hardly images that we associate with empowerment or resistance. The point here is that there is nothing empowering or liberating about speech itself; language in these cases is totally ineffective in either establishing the narrator as a subject whose opinion is worth taking into account or in changing racist practices or speech.

The Woman Warrior continually emphasizes that speaking out against past or present oppressions will not necessarily do anything to ameliorate them. In the chapter "At the Western Palace," Brave Orchid insists that her sister Moon Orchid confront her husband over the fact that he abandoned her decades earlier and that he remarried in the United States. Even though Moon Orchid's husband financially supported her and their daughter, Brave Orchid believes that her sister needs to assert her rights as the first wife over the family, claiming any sons as her own and making her husband and his second wife bend to her will. As Brave Orchid points out, this is what would have been customary in China, and she wants Moon Orchid to seek out revenge for the years that she spent alone in Hong Kong. Moon Orchid, however, has lived a relatively contented and privileged life and has no real interest in seeing her husband again, much less in confronting him about his past actions. Brave Orchid's vociferous insistence that Moon Orchid assert her rights and speak up leads to a disastrous meeting in which the husband (who doesn't seem to have aged) dismisses Moon Orchid and tells her that she is from another life. He is not angry or frightened at her appearance but seems more perturbed. The whole incident causes Moon Orchid to go mad, and as her older sister tells everyone, madness is telling the same story over and over again. Even though we would consider Moon Orchid's confrontation to be liberating, resistant, formative for the constitution of a valorized Asian American subject, it instead just causes Moon Orchid to lose her grip on reality.

Just as often as the book seems to suggest that speech can counter hate, it puts forward the idea that silence can save lives and families, especially when it comes to official channels of power. In a country that excludes the entry of certain groups of people based on a fiction of national identity, the only thing immigrants can do is keep quiet or tell lies:

> We have so many secrets to hold in. . . . There were secrets never to be said in front of the ghosts, immigration secrets whose telling could get us sent back to China. (183)
>
> "Don't tell," advised my parents. "Don't go to San Francisco until they leave."
>
> Lie to Americans. Tell them you were born during the San Francisco earthquake. Tell them your birth certificate and your parents were burned up in the fire. Don't report crimes. . . . Give a new name every time you get arrested; the ghosts won't recognize you. (184)

The narrator's family fears speaking up—to the police, to the government, to their neighbors—precisely because their position as Chinese immigrants makes them vulnerable in ways that others are not. Speech here is not equated with freedom but with imprisonment; to speak up would be to condemn the family.

The critical and popular emphasis on speech and its association with progress and empowerment means that moments of silence within the text go relatively unnoticed. While it is true that the book rails against the silencing of her family when urban renewal paves over the dry-cleaning and laundry business or her own relatively powerlessness in the face of everyday challenges (like interacting with postal workers or bus drivers), it also represents moments when silence is a perfect kind of haven from the slings and arrows of everyday life: "I enjoyed the silence. At first it did not occur to me I was supposed to talk or to pass kindergarten . . . It was when I found out I had to talk that school became a misery. I did not speak and felt bad each time that I did not speak. . . . The other Chinese girls did not talk either, so I knew the silence had to do with being a Chinese girl" (166). Silence can have its own pleasures and power; it is only when speech is enforced that the narrator begins to feel that her silence reflects a lack. The fact that the "silence had to do with being a Chinese girl" suggests that the valorization of speech has as much to do with being a girl in Chinese culture as being Chinese in America. Early in *The Woman Warrior,* the narrator notes that her mother told stories in order to "test our strength to establish realities" (5), but what is abundantly clear as the narrative goes on is that Brave Orchid also uses silence to test her children as well. When her children ask her questions regarding her behavior (e.g., "What do you say when you open the door like that?"), Brave Orchid's response is "'Nothing. . . . It's nothing.' She never explained anything that was really important" (121). After a lifetime of asking questions and never receiving answers, the narrator realizes that "even the good things are unspeakable" and that she and her siblings have to "infer" important occasions based on certain clues (185). While Kingston and her siblings are frustrated by the lack of answers, they don't seem to recognize that their mother is helping them hone their interpretive abilities, even as she denies them easy answers at every turn.

In their final argument at the end of the book, the narrator finally bursts forth with a list of grievances that she has been storing up against her mother. The narrator castigates her mother for always calling her ugly, to which Brave Orchid responds:

> "I didn't say you were ugly."
> "You say that all the time."
> "That's what we're supposed to say. That's what Chinese say. We like to say the opposite."
> It seemed to hurt her to tell me that. (203)

Silence in these moments holds a certain kind of power or knowledge. Speaking one's mind about something important indicates that it's trivial, and it is only by *not* speaking that the importance of a given moment or event or thought is really recognized. We tend to think of the unspeakable as being the tragic or the horrific, but here the unspeakable is what is important or what is precious, what bonds mothers and daughters together. The gulf between what one says and its unspoken "opposite" seems deep but, as Brave Orchid suggests, they can often be one and the same.

Kingston's resistance to the binaries that order our social interactions and politics are on full display in *The Woman Warrior*. Her willingness to challenge the norms of racism and sexism—and even the norms of what we traditionally think of as leftist or liberal politics—means that this text will continue to speak to and infuriate readers. She is determined "not to create singular definitions of ethnic identity to combat the impoverishing stereotypes to which Chinese Americans are subject"; she has no interest in "postulat[ing] the foundations of [any] new hierarchy."[57] Near the start of *The Woman Warrior*, the narrator asks her fellow Chinese Americans, "What is Chinese tradition and what is the movies?" (5–6). At the end of the book, Kingston writes, "I continue to sort out what's my childhood, just my imagination, just my family, just the village, just movies, just living" (205). *The Woman Warrior* provides no answers to the questions it poses but it does suggest that the "sorting out" that often accompanies such queries can be much more productive—and interesting—than any conclusion.

CHAPTER 3

China Men

China Men encompasses many things. It imagines and chronicles the migration and labor stories of generations of men in Kingston's family, including her father. It retells well-known Chinese myths and literary works. It offers brief, fable-like vignettes that seem to straddle the line between history, legend, and personal essay. In one of these vignettes, a Chinese American man lives in a Florida swamp for months on end evading the authorities; in another, Chinese Mandarins find their way to what is now the United States in 1603 via Manila; in still another, a 106-year-old man recounts his memories of Hawai'i starting with his arrival in 1885. Finally *China Men* contains history: two chapters in the middle of the book offer chronologies of dates and facts concerning Chinese migration to the United States. To call it simply a memoir, or a novel, or a history does not do justice to the many kinds of narratives, facts, memories, and fictions it contains. Robert Lee calls *China Men* a "narrative genealogy" made up of "'real' history and hypothesis, live and invented memory."[1] Monica Chiu also emphasizes the book's heterogeneous structure and genre, calling it a "conglomeration of fable, fact, tale, and public policy."[2] I tend to read the book as a scrapbook: a text that contains a mixture of personal memories tied to historical events along with snippets of ideas that seem related in some way to those memories or events.

While these qualities of hybridity, multiplicity, and polyvocality find strong echoes in her other published works, it is Kingston's use of history—or histories—that is one of the distinguishing features of *China Men*. *China Men* chronicles many different kinds of histories: the national histories that we find in textbooks with dates to be memorized and figures (mostly men) to be admired have a place in this book but even more significant are the minor histories, the lost histories, and the imagined histories that Kingston suggests constitute an individual, families, and communities. These are the histories that preoccupy *China Men* the most because these are the histories that have been most overlooked and rendered unworthy of remembrance in the United States. *China Men* is haunted and enthralled by these marginalized and forgotten histories. Reading about the experiences of Chinese men in this work, the reader cannot help but wonder: Why have the stories of the sojourners who journeyed to the United States from China starting almost a century-and-a-half ago been rendered so invisible, unknown, and to a great extent, unknowable? What—if anything—can an author like Kingston do to reclaim those histories? Finally, how can Kingston tell the stories of her ancestors when her readers know so little (if anything) about how and why the men in her family chose to come to and ultimately live and die in the United States?

As *China Men* makes clear, the history of the Chinese in America is also largely a history of labor, and this is a second theme that runs throughout the book. The chapters that focus on the men in the family are ordered generationally (or we could say historically) but also defined by the labor they take on (the narrator's great-grandfather harvests sugarcane, her grandfather builds the railroad, her father works at a gambling house and ultimately owns his own laundry, and her brother teaches in public school before being drafted into the military). Recalling Chinese American history means also recalling the work that Chinese men have performed over the decades, much of it unacknowledged and forgotten but all of it instrumental to the strengthening of the nation.[3] The fact that Kingston originally titled *China Men* as *The Gold Mountain Heroes* suggests that the text is indeed seeking to recognize—even glorify—the contributions of Chinese men who built the country structurally and conceptually, thereby rectifying the wrongs of the past.[4] But the text's treatment of this glorious past is much more complex than one might initially assume. In fact, *China Men* shows how completely impossible it is for Chinese men to gain the posthumous glory that they deserve precisely because the words and experiences of these men can only be reconstructed and not rediscovered. Rather than a recovery of history then, *China Men* is a meditation on loss, and not just the loss of the Hong family but the loss of the hundreds of thousands of Chinese men who toiled and lived anonymously in this country for so many decades.

This chapter will start with an overview of *China Men*, delineating its reception and situating it in relation to *The Woman Warrior* to which it is often (and unfairly) compared. The rest of this chapter will delve into the issues discussed briefly above: the relationship between history, myth, and self; the unacknowledged labor of Chinese men in building the nation; and the power of silence in resisting racism, violence, and exclusion. *China Men* does not offer any easy solutions regarding the historical injustice of Chinese erasure and exclusion. Histories and experiences that have been erased by the passage of time, the inaccessibility of China, and the relentless drive on the part of the United States to disavow the work of its immigrant and racial minorities have insured that. But *China Men* nevertheless suggests that there are ways that Chinese Americans can honor their predecessors without despairing of their deaths or unduly lionizing their lives.

In the Shadow of the Warrior

Given the runaway popularity of *The Woman Warrior,* expectations for *China Men*—on the part of critics and readers—prior to its publication were high and, for the most part, they were met. The book was nearly universally acclaimed; even the critics who lambasted *The Woman Warrior* four years earlier for pandering to white racist ideas of an exotic and inscrutable China remained relatively quiet regarding *China Men,* possibly because they were not as offended by the second book's focus on the men in Kingston's family and its less overtly feminist perspective. Kingston's Chinese American critics were practically the only group not to attempt to compare the two books though. Given the first book's high public profile, and the fact that *China Men* is often thought of as a companion to *The Woman Warrior,* comparisons between *The Women Warrior* and *China Men* were perhaps inevitable. John Leonard, whose original review of *The Woman Warrior* helped vault Kingston to fame, called *China Men* "quite as wonderful as *The Woman Warrior* but angrier." He stated this anger caused "some seams, some scars, in its narratives that were not apparent" in the first book.[5] It is interesting that Leonard ascribes the structural gaps within *China Men* to this "angrier" mode of Kingston's, as if she had less control over her ideas and prose in the second book. This minor critique is leavened by his glowing assessment of Kingston as a writer: "It is, frankly impossible to do justice to Mrs. Kingston's style. If more writers could manage it, our literature would be richer."[6]

Leonard's review was by no means unusual. Noting Kingston's "extraordinary ear for language—not only in riveting visual images but in the recreation of the fractured English and untranslatable puns of her ancestors," Roberta Rubenstein in the *Chicago Tribune* calls *China Men* "another rich lode," in the same "special vein" as *The Woman Warrior.*[7] However, Rubenstein's problematic assertion that reading *China Men* is "like taking a slow boat from China with a superb navigator and guide" and that Kingston serves as a successful "escort . . . through the picturesque, the humorous and the magical" indicates the strength and pervasiveness of the notion that reading Asian American autobiography is—to borrow Sau-ling Wong's phrase—the equivalent of taking a Chinatown tour. Rubinstein's review, with its emphasis on Kingston as Chinese tour guide, was exactly the kind of "misreading" that Kingston railed against in her "Cultural Mis-readings" essay published after *The Woman Warrior.* Phyllis Quan, while praising the book generally, finds the Kingston's insertion of "The Laws" chapter to be "somewhat rude" although "informative." Quan wonders if Kingston possibly "overstates her case by imposing this history lesson on us." She also believes that "The Laws" breaks up the narrative momentum, suggesting that the book never returns to "the bigger-than-life characters whose lives have been crystallized by temporal distance; the second half of the book loses the cohesion and vitality of myth of the first half."[8] Leonard and Quan's notion that the book's insertion of a "history lesson" represents a kind of "seam" or break in the narrative, and their implication that Kingston has somehow lost control of the book, suggests how difficult it can be to narrate Chinese American stories and histories in ways that are legible to mainstream readers.

As this sampling of reviews from national newspapers suggests, *China Men,* while generally lauded and admired, tended to play second fiddle to *The Woman Warrior,* an assessment that continues to this day. Indeed, one of the most popular appraisals about *China Men* is that it balances out the female-focused perspective of *The Woman Warrior.* According to this line of thinking, *China Men* "reflects [Kingston's] balanced treatment of Asian American men's and women's causes" by critiquing racism in America and sexism in China.[9] In other words, *China Men* acts as a corrective to the first book, covering issues and lives that *The Woman Warrior* missed. Whereas *The Woman Warrior* represented Kingston's attempt to understand the women in her family, *China Men* "is impelled by Mrs. Kingston's need to understand the men to whom she is connected: her father, grandfather, brother, mythic figures."[10] Since her male relatives and ancestors did not have a notable presence in that first book, *China Men* offers them a chance to shine.

This sort of understanding of *China Men* as a supplement to a one-sided *The Woman Warrior* sets up both narratives as incomplete without the other. It presumes that a feminist text like *The Woman Warrior* cannot speak for or to the experiences of men, reducing its concerns and politics to the shrill anger of emotionally deadened women. The *Washington Post* in its review of *China Men* expresses surprise that Kingston is able to write of the experiences of her male family members at all given all the feminist rage that must be boiling inside. The reviewer finds it remarkable and refreshing that "in *China Men* Kingston's loyalty to her people has been rekindled and her compassion towards her male forebears outweighs her feminist indignation."[11] This passage exemplifies how feminism is often imagined as being man-hating and "disloyal," devoid of any kind of kindness toward men. The reviewer opines that writing about the men in her family is an indicator that Kingston's "loyalty to her people" and "compassion" have been sparked. This statement implies that *The Woman Warrior* exhibits neither of those qualities, and it ascribes the absence of loyalty and compassion to the fact that the book has an explicitly feminist outlook.

Additionally, this binaristic positioning of *China Men* vis-à-vis *The Woman Warrior* portrays *China Men* as somehow less polyvocal and more conventionally historical than its predecessor. Such interpretations also tend to position *China Men* as the antifeminist, man-glorifying text in opposition to *The Woman Warrior.* It becomes the binary opposite of the earlier, more well-known and well-read book. But that binaristic understanding of Kingston's first two works does not begin to encompass the complexities with which *China Men* grapples. As King-Kok Cheung and other critics have noted, *China Men* is just as ambivalent about issues of gender as it is about issues regarding ethnic and racial identity. Maureen Sabine in her work examining *The Woman Warrior* and *China Men* argues that critics have imposed a "gender separatist" reading method that emphasizes the daughter's relationship to her mother in *The Woman Warrior* but at the expense of her relationship with her father and other men in her family in *China Men.*[12] She argues that rather than thinking about the two books as expressing oppositional tendencies, it might be more fruitful to consider them as intertexts: speaking to and across each other. While it is outside the scope of this book to situate *The Woman Warrior* and *China Men* intertextually, such an analysis no doubt would acknowledge the complications and contradiction within each book and across both books.

To be fair, Kingston herself has at times promoted the notion that *China Men* can only be understood when placed in relation to *The Woman Warrior.* Kingston has spoken of *The Woman Warrior* and *China Men* as "one big book. I was writing them more or less simultaneously. The final chapter in *China Men* began as a short story that I was working on before I even started *The Woman Warrior.*"[13] The stories of the male ancestors in her family "seemed to interfere" with *The Woman Warrior*'s feminist perspective; they were, as Kingston put it, "weakening the feminist point of view. So I took all the men's stories out."[14] In another interview, Kingston discussed the fact that she thinks of "*China Men* [as] a sequel to [*The*] *Woman Warrior.* I see each book as building on the last one. It's almost like I do the rewrites and then the next book is another rewrite."[15] Kingston's images—first, of one book split in two because the components of the second weakened the structure of the first, and second, of *China Men* as a rewrite of *The Woman Warrior*—has informed many of the responses toward *China Men.* This understanding of the relationship between the two works sets up *China Men* as a foil to *The Woman Warrior.* Whereas *The Woman Warrior* is a text about women, *China Men* is about men. *The Woman Warrior* traffics in ambiguity; *China Men* is about the law. *The Woman Warrior* explores the effects of gender oppression; *China Men* concerns itself with anti-Chinese racism. *The Woman Warrior* is the feminist text while *China Men* is the ethnic text.[16]

Despite these easy characterizations, it quickly becomes evident that *China Men* is as full of textual ellipses, ambiguities, lost stories, and silences as *The Woman Warrior.* For example, one of the early and recurring themes of the book is that there are multiple stories for how her father entered the United States. As Kingston herself noted in an interview, "in the course of [*China Men*], I have [my father] coming into this country in five different ways. I'm very proud of that."[17] Part of the reason for the proliferating immigration stories is because her father entered illegally, and even decades after his arrival, she feels classic second-generation immigrant paranoia about running afoul of the law. As in *The Woman Warrior,* there is an injunction against speaking, although in this case, that injunction has the force of the law behind it. But there's also a commonality between Kingston and her father: "If [my father] has the freedom to tell four stories about himself, then I have the freedom, as a writer, to give my versions too."[18] Despite all of the restrictions that have circumscribed their lives and never allowed them to feel completely comfortable in this country, both Kingston and her father are "free" when they tell stories. While fear of government intervention has effectively prevented the family from knowing the whole story of her father's arrival in the United States, Kingston has no such fear of literary purists who constantly seek to categorize and classify her narratives. Having been silenced in one way, Kingston refuses to be silenced in another.

The Layer Cake

As I mentioned at the start of the chapter, *China Men* is comprised of three different types of layered narratives. The first type consist of six long chapters that focus on the narrator's ancestors, the men who came to the United States first as laborers and then as immigrants and finally as citizens: two great-grandfathers who worked the sugarcane fields in Hawai'i in the mid-nineteenth century; her grandfather who helped build the Transcontinental Railroad in the 1860s; her father who was a scholar in China but decided to try his luck on Gold Mountain because he hated being a schoolteacher; and finally her brother, who chose to fight in Vietnam even though he opposed the war. The second narrative type is made up of Kingston's reimaginings of Chinese myths, legends, and history. The third narrative type is the most difficult to define easily and consists of the shortest chapters—usually only a few pages. These chapters tend to contain brief, anecdotal vignettes from the narrator's life or strange stories—somewhere between myth and gossip—that she has read or heard about. Kingston describes *China Men* as "a six-layer cake and the myths are like icing."[19] Choosing another metaphor to describe the book's structure, Roorbach claims that "the sections of *China Men* resembl[e] facets of a great jewel, which Kingston turns and turns, showing the reader more, and then more again, in hopes that he or she comes to understand the human enormity that is the Chinese-American psyche."[20] The first three chapters of *China Men* exemplify Roorbach's claim that the different types of narratives that make up *China Men* reveals facets of the others. These chapters consist of a short vignette from the narrator's past, a retelling of an eighteenth-century Chinese novel, and the story of the narrator's father's move from China to the United States. These chapters blend intensely personal family memories with the national and global histories that propel family members all over the world as well as the mythical stories of a China to which the narrator has no direct access. How can the reader make sense of the relationship between the multiple types of narratives in *China Men:* the brief vignettes of her family life, the retellings of Chinese myth, and the stories of her ancestors journeying, laboring, and living in the United States? If each type of narrative is a layer, what is the relationship between the various layers to each other? And what do they say about the China Men who are the eponymous heroes?

The notion that the various types of chapters are layers that build upon each other, even as they maintain their own distinct characteristics, gives us a clue as to how to understand the relationship between the various types of narratives. Family histories, legends, rumors—each type of narrative individually cannot begin to encompass the complexities of Chinese American experience, but when they are juxtaposed with each other, they do reveal how fractured the Chinese American experience has been and continues to be. In other words, these layers don't unite the pieces of Chinese America into a coherent whole but rather highlight how fragmented that history is. The seams and breaks in *China Men* that give critics Leonard and Quan pause do not stem from anger on Kingston's part but are rather constitutive to Chinese American narratives themselves.

In her review of *China Men,* cited above, Phyllis Quan makes particular mention of "The Laws" chapter in the middle of the book, questioning its purpose and wondering whether it breaks up the narrative in such a way that the second half of the text is disconnected from the first. Structurally speaking, Quan is right to point out what an outlier "The Laws" is to *China Men,* and one might even argue, to Kingston's oeuvre as a whole. Sandwiched in the exact center of *China Men,* this chapter provides a history of the Chinese in America with important events presented in chronological order by year and described briefly in the neutral and passive prose of an encyclopedia entry. The chapter starts with the year 1868 and the Burlingame Treaty, which was supposed to recognize the rights of the Chinese to migrate to the United States for the "purposes of curiosity, of trade, or as permanent residents," to 1978, when US immigration laws were changed to allow for the immigration of 290,000 people annually, with about 22,000 Chinese entering legally that year. "The Laws" chapter is totally unique in Kingston's work. For one thing, it contains no descriptive or literary language; it is dry, official, and heavily focused on dates and major events. For another thing, it contains no references to the narrator's family nor is there any attempt to connect it to what precedes it or what follows. There is no preamble to the chapter, no footnotes to clue the reader into its purpose, and no comment within the book explaining either the form the chapter takes or why Kingston felt its inclusion was necessary.

Only in interviews has Kingston described her rationale for including what amounts to a history timeline in the center of her narrative: "The mainstream culture doesn't know the history of Chinese Americans which has been written and written well. That ignorance makes a tension for me, and in the new book I just couldn't take it anymore. So all of a sudden, right in the middle of the stories, plunk—there is an eight-page section of pure history. . . . It really affects the shape of the book, and it might look quite clumsy. But on the other hand, maybe it will affect the shape of the novel in the future. Now maybe another Chinese American writer won't have to write that history."[21] Kingston presents "The Laws" as a quick and dirty corrective to what she perceives as her readers' lack of knowledge about Chinese American history. Her rhetoric that she "couldn't take it anymore" and that "The Laws" was "plunk[ed]" down impulsively and without consideration as to how it might affect the rest of the book suggests a writing process that is unstructured, free-flowing, and organic. In these comments, Kingston elides the work of revision that must accompany fiction-writing, instead presenting herself as someone who writes down ideas as they come to her. However, Kingston acknowledges almost immediately that the inclusion of "The Laws" "might look quite clumsy." Kingston states that her purpose is to spare future Chinese American writers the frustration of writing for a readership that doesn't have a basic knowledge about American history, but by plunking "The Laws" into the middle of *China Men* Kingston emphasizes how Chinese Americans *lack* a historical record and the problems that come about when history cannot be remembered or reclaimed. The inclusion of some dates and events hardly makes up for the centuries of erasure that the Chinese in American have endured. In that sense, the entire book is a history, not just the chapters that contain straightforward historical fact. Kingston states that "I saw *China Men* as a history book, and it would be a story that has been left out of history, the migrations coming from China, the migrations to America that came from the east and not from Europe."[22] "The Laws," far from rendering it unnecessary for readers to know more about Chinese American history and experiences, instead reveals the paucity of information available and how little of that can be recovered at all. The abrupt inclusion of these chapters in *China Men* emphasizes the violence of the erasure of the Chinese from American historical narratives.

"The Laws" also highlights the constitutive relationship between the law and Asian American identity. For Kandice Chuh and Karen Shimakawa "The Laws" chapter indicates "the challenges [that] legal conditions [such as exclusion] have posed to the belongingness and life chances of Chinese immigrants and Chinese Americans."[23] They go on to claim that by making "The Laws" the core of the book, Kingston is emphasizing how those laws are at the core of Asian American identity: "Kingston emphasizes how US law has functioned to produce Asian Americans as categorically different from the exemplary American and illustrates the material effects of this production on the lives and psyches of those so categorized."[24] In other words, Chinese American identity emerged from and was indelibly formed by the welter of exclusion laws, antimiscegenation ordinances, restrictive covenants, and other legislative and legal prohibitions directed against the Chinese that were enacted on the federal, state, and local level. One cannot talk about a Chinese American subject or community without referencing this long history of exclusion, and *China Men* makes that clear by "plunking" "The Laws" in the center of the text.

The extent to which the histories of erasure and exclusion play into the personal experiences and movements of the Chinese American family can be seen early in *China Men,* when the narrator talks about her dream to go to China if only she can convince her family it would be safe to do so. Her family is "afraid that applying for a visa would call attention to us: the relatives in China would get in trouble for having American capitalist connections, and we Americans would be put in relocation camps during the next witch hunt for Communist" (84).

In one paragraph, the narrator demonstrates how the interactions between nations (the United States and China) not only reflect the geopolitics of neo-imperialism and the Cold War but also intersects with her own family's sense of themselves as Chinese living in the United States. Years of living under repressive and unjust immigration and citizenship laws means that her family is completely suspicious of US bureaucracy. Given the internment of Japanese Americans during World War II and the anti-Communist hysteria and witch hunts of the McCarthy Era, it is not surprising that Chinese Americans would not view the United States as the land of opportunity and individual freedom that it so often imagines itself to be. On the other hand, years of receiving letters from desperate relatives and hearing rumors from within their community about the brutality of the Maoist regime in China have made them fearful of returning to China and becoming pawns in the Cold War between the United States and China. What seems initially like paranoia at first glance is quickly revealed to be completely an understandable and justifiable fear after reviewing the history between the two countries.

"Should I be able to convince my family about the good will of normalization, it is not the Great Wall I want to see but my ancestral village. I want to talk to Cantonese, who have always been revolutionaries, nonconformists, people who invented the Gold Mountain. I want to discern what it is that makes people go West and turn into Americans. I want to compare China, a country I made up, with what country is really out there." (85)

Even if she is able to overcome these concerns, the narrator has no interest in visiting the Great Wall or the China she sees in travel brochures. Rather, she wants to visit the "ancestral village" from which her father, mother, and family sprung and to see if China, "the country I made up," matches up with the China that is "really" there (84). Kingston writes that her Cantonese villagers are known to be "revolutionaries [and] nonconformists" who "invented Gold Mountain" (84). It is this notion—that despite being forgotten by history, the men of these villages created and built Gold Mountain—that runs counter to all kinds of American foundational myths. America in this case was not founded by the white slave-owning elite class who refused to pay taxes to an empire but rather by Kingston's own villagers and ancestors, who harvested cash crops, built the railroad, and believed in the economic possibilities that America represented even before the nation itself.

China Men offers a different way of thinking about history. In its attempt to explore Chinese American identity in the face of historical loss, the book revamps or revises the way that "history" as a category of narration is constructed and read. By intermixing her own family's story with history as it is traditionally understood, Kingston destabilizes the binary between the official history that define nation-states and the highly rhizomatic and particular histories that make up a family's experience. What is more, Kingston questions the very distinction that tends to separate the historical from the personal. As Leilani Nishime contends, "In *China Men* rather than attempting to rid Chinese-American history of the 'taint' of the personal or autobiographical, Kingston revises notions of what makes an experience historical, by asking by what standards we decide what can enter into history and the public realm."[25]

Caroline Yang makes a similar claim when she argues that *China Men* is concerned with "not only how history gets narrated and who is left out in the construction of a national history but also how certain workers and their work are persistently overlooked."[26] The lives of these overlooked Chinese men cannot be rewritten or recovered, although we can still see the fruits of their labor. Trying to renarrate their lives or imagine what they may have gone through cannot recapture or compensate the men, their labor, or their lives. *China Men* makes no claim that its attempt to make the struggles of these men visible at least through text can offer any kind of real recompense to the traumas that these men endured.

The text does, however, make an effort to at least make these losses palpable through its structure. King-Kok Cheung argues that Kingston's portrayal of the Tang Ao myth that opens *China Men* mythologizes the history of Chinese men in the "New World." The story that Kingston briefly tells is derived from an eighteenth-century Chinese novel called *Flowers in the Mirror.* Tang Ao, the protagonist, is captured in the Land of Women; his capture initially seems like it will be a romantic boon (the narrator notes wryly "if he had had male companions, he would've winked over his shoulder" upon being led away by the women), but he is quickly and efficiently forced to undergo a series of bodily transformations in order to become a beautiful woman: his feet are broken and bound, his ears are pierced with a needle, his hair is plucked, and his face is painted. Tang Ao is also forced to participate in his humiliation by his captors as he is required to wash the bandages that wrap his feet; he is ashamed of them when he hangs them to dry as they look like underwear.

By locating the Land of Women in North America, Kingston is clearly commenting on the emasculation and physical torment that Chinese men endured during their time in the United States. But as Cheung notes, the gender commentary in this story is a double-edged sword, for the story, with its descriptions of the kinds of physical torture and mutilation that women have endured for centuries, also reveals the "subjugation of women both in old China and in America. . . . Her myth deplores on the one hand the racist debasement of Chinese American men and [on the] other hand the sexist objectification of Chinese women."[27] Cheung's reading makes clear that the "either/or" dynamic that is shot through commentary on *China Men,* especially as it relates to *The Woman Warrior,* only gets half of the story. Even though Kingston is exploring the "meaning of China Men's marginality in white-centered America," she retains, as Shu-mei Shih argues, a feminist perspective.[28]

While the relationship between the chapters chronicling the men in the narrator's family and the chapters retelling Chinese myths seems to be a part of this dynamic in which history and History are mingled, less clear is what purpose the short anecdotal chapters—some narrated in first person and others not—have. The chapters that make up this third layer of the narrative are perhaps the most difficult to characterize or categorize. Shu-mei Shih argues that the short chapters that are interspersed throughout the work serve as intertexts to the other chapters that deal specifically with the narrator's family. These intertextual connections highlight the trope of exile, which Shih argues is at the heart of the Chinese American experience. Shih's emphasis on exile contrasts with Chuh and Shimakawa's emphasis on legal discourse as central to the experiences of Chinese Americans. The representation of exile in these interchapters is often suggestive rather than explicit and is illustrated as a form of misrecognition rather than an unambiguous loss of or longing for home. For example, the first of these short chapters—which is also the first chapter in the book—describes how the narrator and her siblings run to greet their father coming home from work only to realize that the man they are embracing and clamoring over is *not* their father. Curiously, the narrator responds to the man's assertion that he is not their father by agreeing that "he *probably* was not" (7, emphasis added). When another man turns the corner "one finger touching his hat to salute us," the children run to meet him, but the chapter ends before we know definitively if this man is truly their father or another case of misidentification. The dream-like quality to this chapter, in which a child cannot positively identify her father and must rely on others to help her make her determination, indicates the fragility of the paternal relationship and foreshadows the difficulties the daughter has in connecting to her father and his past in the rest of the book.

These fraught paternal relations are the backdrop for the last chapter in *China Men*. The chapter consists of dinner party conversation between the narrator, a "Filipino scholar," and "a group of Chinese Americans" (308). The scholar tells a story about three Chinese Mandarins who "came to the Philippines to look for the Gold Mountain" in 1603. Due to the late hour, the accent of the speaker, and the noise of the party, the narrator finds it difficult to understand what the scholar is saying and asks him to clarify his comments, which surprisingly do not seem to make the story any more comprehensible. The narrator asks the scholar to repeat his tale, and he responds that he will write everything down in a letter and "mail it to you." The narrator responds "Good. Now I could watch the young men who listen." Given the fact that the entire book is about her struggle to listen to her father and the voices of her Chinese ancestors who have been lost to history, there is pleasure for the narrator in asking for a story about Chinese American forbearers and hearing multiple versions of that story. She also relishes the opportunity to stand back and watch other men talk and "listen." As Kingston has wryly noted, talking has never been her mother's or her problem, but to "hear the silent men of Kingston's heritage, especially over the ebullient talk-story of the women in Kingston's life, she must listen; we all must listen."[29]

Labor

As indicated throughout this chapter, a central concern of *China Men* is to chronicle the labor of Chinese men, labor that the book considers foundational to the growth of the United States into a global empire and has been completely forgotten in terms of this country's rise. That labor is one of the important tropes of *China Men* should come as no surprise; after all, the men in Kingston's family came to the United States for one reason and one reason alone: to work and make enough money to send back to their war- and drought-stricken country. There is nothing romantic about the work that is depicted here: it is back-breaking, humiliating, and dangerous. Even when the work is not physical labor per se but the labor of teaching, it is portrayed as being a slog and thankless grind, robbed of any idealism, intellectual stimulation, or altruistic significance. Both the narrator's father and her brother are teachers, and *China Men* is not an advertisement for the joys of being an educator. The narrator's brother—based on an amalgamation of Kingston's own brothers, two of whom served in Vietnam—teaching in California high schools, challenges his students to think of ways to stop the war in Vietnam; in response, they accuse him of being a Communist or "gookish" (279). He discovers that the books that he has bought for his English class with his own funds have been defaced by the students: "Somebody had jammed books behind the radiator and up the air vent, 'Fuck you, basturds' scrawled on their pages. Books that he had bought for a classroom library were ripped in half along the bindings" (279). Similarly, the narrator's father, a village school teacher in China, assumes that his students will have the same love of learning and poetry that he has; upon realizing that they do not respect him because he does not teach them in the same rote manner that is expected in the school room, he begins to fear that being around them is making him stupider: "The students ruined his eating; they ruined his sleep. They spoiled the songs of birds. And they were taking his books and calligraphy from him too—no time for his own reading, no time to practice his own writing. Teaching was destroying his literacy" (39). Baba longs for physical labor, which he romanticizes as working in a field of rice with its "quiet surprises," filled with mushrooms, eggs, and lilies (41). The risks of Gold Mountain are more appealing to him than another moment spent in the schoolroom.

All of these men, from the great-grandfather to the brother, perform their work with honor and dignity, even when they disagree with it or are treated badly by the men and companies who oversee their work. While the text portrays the brother in Vietnam as the conscience of a nation that seems to have abandoned its own, the majority of the book is taken up with the lives and labors of the men whom the narrator cannot access: her great-grandfather, grandfather, and, to a lesser extent, her father. Bak Goong, the narrator's great-grandfather, is the oldest familial figure that the narrator focuses on, the first in the family to travel to Gold Mountain. Ironically, he does not come to America to seek out gold but rather as coolie labor for the sugarcane fields in Hawaii. The process of planting the sugarcane is taxing, and harvesting requires the men to set the fields on fire and breathe in the smoke and fumes while they work. The Chinese men are like animals, driven to work no matter what their physical condition. They cannot express their anger or homesickness directly, but they find ways to articulate their feelings of loneliness and rage. Sugarcane is not the only thing that the China Men are planting. Bak Goong leads his fellow sugarcane workers in digging holes in the earth and screaming into them in order to dispel their resentment and frustration at their work conditions.

> "I want home," Bak Goong yelled, pressed against the soil, and smelling the earth. "I want my home," the men yelled together, "I want home. Home. Home. Home. Home."
>
> Talked out, they buried their words, planted them. (117–18)

The image of "planting" of course invokes the familiar trope of "putting down roots," a phrase that suggests that one has found or is establishing a home. The roots in this case do not symbolize stability, welcome, or domesticity; rather they are planting their anger, bitterness, and longing for "home" within United States soil. This notion of burying their words means that there is a possibility that someone in later generations can unearth them, call them forward, or that like seeds, they will eventually sprout into something whether for good or bad. It also suggests that anger—over their exile, over their exploitation, over their exclusion—is at the root of the experiences of the Chinese in the United States.

Despite the anger that the China Men feel toward their overseers and bosses, they exhibit a connection to the land that they are being forced to burn and pillage. In fact, the act of shouting into the ground unburdens the men, offering them an outlet for their powerlessness. This notion that the land and environment can somehow console the China Men may seem contradictory, given that their attempts to domesticate the land for cultivation are so difficult. Kingston describes how her great-grandfather's lungs burn with the harvesting of the sugarcane and how their bodies are abused by overseers determined to wring as much work out of them as possible. But the narrative makes clear that the China Men and the land are not enemies and that the land can even provide solace and an outlet for the men's frustrations and anger. For example, Bak Goong "pats the pregnant earth" after seeding it, a gesture that suggests that although the men are breaking themselves to tame and cultivate the land, the land itself is not the cause of their suffering (101). And while the dust and smoke that Bak Goong breathes in from the smoldering sugarcane chokes and suffocates him, it also "come[s] in handy" as it offers him the opportunity to express his fury in ways that cannot be deciphered by the "white demons": "When the demons howled to work faster, faster, he coughed in reply. The deep, long, loud coughs, barking and wheezing, were almost as satisfying as shouting. He let out scolds disguised as coughs. When the demon beat his horse and dust rose from its brown flanks, he coughed from his very depths. All Chinese words conveniently a syllable each, he said, 'Get—that—horse—dust—away—from—me—you—dead—white—demon. Don't—stare—at—me—with—those—glass—eyes. I—can't—take—this—life.' He felt better after having his say. He did not even mind the despair, which dispelled upon his speaking it" (104). As his body breaks down, Bak Goong transforms it into an instrument of anger and resistance. He cannot shout as it would attract the attention of the "demons," but his cough—usually considered a sign of weakness or contamination—is the sign of his defiance.

Most important, Bak Goong insists that his presence and the presence of the other China Men in the United States means that they were more than witnesses to the building of the nation—they actually were instrumental in establishing it. When some of the China Men suggest that they practice of yelling into the ground is a Chinese custom, Bak Goong retorts "That wasn't a custom. . . . We made it up. We can make up customs because we're the founding ancestors of this place" (117–18). Later in the text, the narrator states that her father is lured to Gold Mountain not just based on the wealth that he thinks he can find there but also because "gold blood ran in [his family's] veins. How could they not to go the Gold Mountain again, which belonged to them, which they had invented and discovered?" (43). This image that Gold Mountain runs through the veins of the Hong men upends the customary and racist belief that the Chinese are perpetual foreigners in the United States because of their racial difference. The blood of America runs through their veins; they belong to it as much as anyone else. This rhetoric of Chinese "invention" and "discovery" counters Western histories that have always emphasized the European "discovery" of the Americas—Kingston suggests that conceptually, the Chinese arrived first. *China Men* demands that the nation recognize not just Chinese contributions to America but also the foundational role that the Chinese had in establishing the nation and its national myths. Before newcomers from Europe dreamed of seeing Lady Liberty in New York harbor, before America had a reputation for being a nation of immigrants, the Chinese conceived of this country that way. They invented the America of the American Dream before the nation itself. That's why the text places so much emphasis on the notion that the Chinese "invented" America—they may not have been the first to arrive (although Kingston refutes that idea even in the last chapter of *China Men*) but they were among the first to see what America *could* be.

Kingston makes her strongest case for the foundational role of the Chinese in building the notion through the railroad, particularly the Transcontinental Railroad, which is what her own grandfather worked on. He was not alone. The first track for what would become the Transcontinental was laid down in 1863, with the Central Pacific Railroad building eastward from Sacramento and the Union Pacific building westward from Council Bluffs, Iowa. The two tracks met in 1869 at Promontory Point, Utah, with the ceremonial driving of the "Golden Spike," an event that is immortalized in a famous photograph of the same name. A small number of Chinese men were initially hired in 1865 by the Central Pacific in anticipation of a strike; the company found that despite their smaller stature in comparison to their white counterparts, they were better and—more important—cheaper workers. The Central Pacific began hiring Chinese in droves in 1865 and sending out recruiters to lure more Chinese to the railroad camps. Although it is impossible to know the exact number of Chinese who worked on the Transcontinental, some historians have estimated that between ten and fifteen thousand Chinese men were involved, although these numbers may be too low.[30] By the time the final rail had been laid, Chinese workers comprised twelve thousand of the fifteen thousand workers on the Central Pacific payroll.[31] They laid down the track for the most treacherous portion of the railroad—over the Sierras—and were often called upon to do the most dangerous work of using dynamite and then nitroglycerin to blast out the rock. The physically backbreaking and emotionally taxing nature of this work was made all the more difficult by the inhospitable physical conditions and the poor pay the Chinese received especially in comparison to their white counterparts.

Despite this—or perhaps because of this—Kingston argues that these Chinese men not only built the country but also bound it together into a lasting union: "They built railroads in every part of the country—the Alabama and Chattanooga Railroad, the Houston and Texas Railroad, the Southern Pacific, the railroads in Louisiana and Boston, the Pacific Northwest, and Alaska. After the Civil War, China Men banded the nation North and South, East and West, with crisscrossing steel. They were the binding and building ancestors of this place" (146). This rhetoric that the Chinese are the ancestors, the founding fathers of America is not just based on the fact that they arrived here but is also because they *worked* here. They harvested sugarcane, they built the railroad, they mined gold, and then, they built laundries, worked restaurants, and farmed. If the railroad transformed the United States into an imagined community, the work of the Chinese on the Transcontinental and other railroads laid the foundation for that community.

The intertwining of railroad, Chinese Americans, and her own family is deepened by Kingston's description of the relationship between her grandfather to the railroad he is building. Ah Goong built the railroad but he also fathered the railroad. Dangled from a basket onto a sheer rockface in order to position explosives, Ah Goong finds himself overwhelmed by physical desire. Shooting ejaculate onto the valley floor below, Ah Goong imagines that he is "fucking the world." Whenever he is lowered in the basket thenceforth, "his blood rushed to his penis, and he fucked the world" (133). Monica Chiu writes that "nowhere in *China Men* is labor redemptive," but I would suggest that there are moments in the book when labor—when it is defined outside of the parameters of capitalist production—can be, if not redemptive, than certainly satisfying.[32] Here Kingston plays upon the two meanings of "labor" as indicating work but also indicating birth. Kingston's representation of the railroad as emerging from the ground where Ah Goong spills his seed emphasizes not only what Ah Goong gave in order to "birth" the Transcontinental but also how tightly the railroad is intertwined into the Hong family tree; so tightly that it is almost like a child to Ah Goong. The railroad is not just a material object that was manufactured by Chinese men, it carries the DNA of the Chinese men who built it.

As I have argued elsewhere, Ah Goong's sexual arousal "speaks obliquely to the impact that strict anti-miscegenation laws and anti-immigration laws prohibiting the legal entry of Chinese women had on Chinese men in the U.S."[33] His erection is the result of the beauty that surrounds him as well as the fear brought on by his work and anxiety about ever seeing his home and family again. Gary Okihiro argues that Ah Goong's "masculine thrust" is an "exercise in futility" because his semen falls on a barren ground, that is, because it does not result in reproduction.[34] Similarly David Li suggests that Ah Goong's masturbatory act indicates his lack of "political [or] economic mastery over the land" upon which he is building.[35] Both critics see Ah Goong's sex act as an expression of his impotence, politically and reproductively. But it seems to me that Okihiro's and Li's readings impose a heterosexist ideal upon the Chinese laborers, one which valorizes traditional and patriarchal notions of male sexuality and fatherhood. Ah Goong's act is one that deliberately falls out of the controls of a reproductive economy that is otherwise hell-bent on extracting the most value from workers as possible. He is supposed to be working—inserting explosives into the cliff face in order to blast out tunnels for the railroad—but there is really no time when he is free of the Central Pacific's watch: he eats when they feed him, sleeps where they set up the camps, and works the rest of the time. Even though he is ostensibly on the company's clock, this is one of the few times where the railroad company cannot control what he is doing. "Fucking the world" is not an act of impotence; it is one of joyful rebellion against the temporal and physical controls imposed by the nation and its proxies.

Ah Goong's sexual act is thus productive even if it isn't *re*productive. From Ah Goong's spilled seed comes the railroad itself. The scene between Ah Goong and the Sierras adds to the mythic sense of the Chinese American story. Ah Goong's terraphilia produces the Transcontinental Railroad, just as in myth gods sleep with the earth and produce other gods. This anecdote is not just history and it is not just a family story; it is also part of a legend. That sense of labor and legend is echoed in the final part of the chapter in which the narrator talks about how as a result of the San Francisco earthquake and its ensuing fire, Ah Goong is able to have a child: "He had built the railroad out of sweat, why not have an American child out of longing?" (151). Just as he and his father conceived and therefore founded America, Ah Goong is able to will into existence a family of his own. This kind of mythical birth is part of the family's own legend, and represents a mingling of national myths with familial ones. For example, at the start of the chapter "The American Father," the narrator announces that "in 1903 my father was born in San Francisco, where my grandmother had come disguised as a man" (238). She follows this statement with another, even more impossible story for her father's birth: that her father's mother gave birth in China and sent her son to his father in San Francisco because, as the narrator laconically puts it, "She was good at sending" (238). The next sentence contains another impossible origin story: that her own grandfather had the ability to give birth to babies. Not only do these statements directly contradict earlier accounts of the father's arrival in the United States via crate from Cuba but they also suggest that her father's entrance into the United States was dramatic and fantastic at the same time. The various images of birth that *China Men* depicts—of a grandfather emerging from the flames of destruction with a baby of his own, of a father born to mother disguised as a man, or children being conceived when the parents are far away from each other—suggest the constructed nature of family narratives. These multiple and contradictory stories about origins and birth are the direct result of Chinese exclusion laws; they reflect the injustices that the Chinese faced in the United States but also the ingenuity and creativity they showed in resisting those injustices.

Despite all of the obstacles the Chinese face during the construction of the railroad—the dangerous conditions, the unequal pay, the loneliness and deprivation—the China Men express their pleasure and pride when the work is completed. Even if their work on the railroad was appropriated by white men and corporations, the fruits of their labor are still worth celebrating. In describing the scene in which the Union Pacific and Central Pacific tracks are finally joined together in Promontory Point, Utah, in 1869, Kingston notes that the "China Men cheered. . . . They Yippee'd like madmen" (145). While the Chinese laborers celebrated their Herculean accomplishment, the "white demon officials gave speeches" in which they proclaimed that the completion of the Transcontinental Railroad was "The Greatest Feat in the History of Mankind" and that "Only Americans could have done it" (145). The narrator concedes that the last point was true but not in the way that the "white demons" meant. The narrator's definition of who the Americans are in this instance is entirely different than the Americans the "white demons" are thinking of. Building the railroad *made* Ah Goong and the other China Men American. With the driving in of the final spike, China Men earned their place in America as citizens. The mention here of Ah Goong's citizenship—which some Chinese men were able to obtain from local officials before the passage of the Chinese Exclusion Act in 1882—emblematizes Hutcheon's point that in *China Men* "documents are shown to be extremely unstable sources of identity: American citizenship papers, visas, and passports are all bought and sold with ease."[36] The existence of the railroad proves, more than the "Citizenship Papers" purchased by Ah Goong from some fraudulent judge, that he belongs in the United States.

Speech and Silence Redux

The fact that there is no written record for her to examine, no paper trail of papers, visas, and passports for her to peruse, means that narrator of *China Men* does not know many important points in her family's history. This was also the case in *The Woman Warrior* but in that text, the narrator was dealing with a parent who was loquacious and often produced multiple versions of the same story. The narrator recognizes in herself a similar love for words. Whereas the narrator and her mother love to talk, the father is, in contrast, silent. Early in *China Men,* the narrator reveals that she resembles MaMa insofar as they both have "peasant minds. We see a stranger's tic and ascribe motives" (15). This desire to unravel the unknown and to interpret signs bind the narrator and her mother together—we can certainly see that in multiple instances in *The Woman Warrior.* The narrator, however, does not share this characteristic with her father. She tells her father that she will interpret stories from "your silences and few words, and you can tell me that I'm mistaken. You'll just have to speak up with the real stories if I've got you wrong" (15). Rather than being reinterpretations of stories she has already been told, the stories about the narrator's father in *China Men* will be based on all the things that her father doesn't tell her.

What her father cannot or will not say is what most troubles the narrator. The narrator often considers her father's silences to be menacing, a sign of his detachment from and resentment toward his children. After a run-in with a cheating laundry customer triggers a visit from the police, the children are "careful not to be bad or noisy so that you [their father] would not turn on us. We knew that it was to feed us you had to endure demons and physical labor" (13). The words that he does utter in these moments and after are rife with violence, an inarticulate rage that does not express his anger so much as stoke it. The guilt that the children have for the humiliations their father has to endure does not make his anger any less terrifying. He swears daily at his customers, particularly the "gypsy women" who try to cheat him. "Dog vomit" he calls them, "stink pig," and worse. The narrator fervently hopes that his misogynistic imprecations are not directed toward all women or the women in the family. She longs to hear him say "Those were only sayings. . . . I didn't mean your mother or grandmothers or women in general" (14). The unspoken element of that list is "or you." His nightmares jolt him out of sleep with "wordless male screams" (13), implying that while females articulate their anguish (as they did in *The Woman Warrior*), men either cannot or will not.

The few instances in which he does speak, however, reveals how powerful his words, carefully chosen, can be. For example, when the police raid the gambling house where he worked and arrest him, BaBa tells his daughter he never gave his own real name. "[The police] never found out his real names or that he had an American name at all. 'I got away with aliases,' he said, 'because the white demons can't tell one Chinese name from another or one face from another.' He had the power of naming" (242). This power to name extends to the narrator's own name, which was taken from a "blonde gambler who always won. [Your father] gave you her lucky American name" (243). Importantly, it is not the narrator's father who reveals this bit of information about the narrator's name to the narrator but her mother. The narrator seems to suggest that in the case of her father, speech has power only when it is juxtaposed with silence.

This power to name seems to complement the other power that the narrator ascribes to her father: the "power of going places where nobody else went, and making places belong to him" (238). The narrator says that she can "smell his presence" in spaces that he has chosen for his own: "He owned special places the way he owned special things like his copper ashtray from the 1939 World's Fair, and his Parker 51. When I explored his closet and desk, I thought, This is a father place, a father belongs here" (238). The narrator's father also chose his own name (which is translated into English as "Think Virtue") and as the narrator notes, it "brought him enough luck and so he kept it" (29). But the power to name or to speak does not make one a less vulnerable national subject. The narrator refuses to reveal her father's full name because she is afraid that such information will lead to his deportation (since he arrived in the country illegally). The idea that her father is powerful and yet still subject of the whims of a vast bureaucratic state—these two contradictory ideas are in constant tension throughout Kingston's oeuvre. The narrator understands her father's power to name as one that is always formed within the confines of the exclusion laws and police powers of the state.

While his screams and rants terrify his children, even worse are his silences, which the narrator thinks of as punishment: "You rendered us invisible, gone" (14). There is a power to patriarchal silence. In *The Woman Warrior,* Brave Orchid forbids the narrator from speaking and often confuses her children by choosing not to explain the important things in life—because speech somehow cheapens the feelings or traditions of the family. But in *China Men,* BaBa's unwillingness or inability to communicate makes the children feel like they simply do not exist. In order to understand their BaBa, the children create stories about him to explain his silence: "You kept up a silence for weeks and months. We invented the terrible things that you were thinking: That your mother had done you some unspeakable wrong, and so you left China forever. That you hate daughters. That you hate China" (14). None of these things, it turns out, are true, but they are the only explanations the children can formulate to explain their father's silence. BaBa's taciturnity is emphasized by the fact that there is little material relating to him within the family's archive. While the narrator talks of seeing her mother's old diploma from medical school and school pictures in *The Woman Warrior,* in this text there is no such record of her father's Chinese life in the family home. She states that her father only "look[s] and talk[s] Chinese. There are no photographs of you in Chinese clothes nor against Chinese landscapes. Did you cut your pigtail to show your support for the Republic? Or have you always been American? Do you mean to give us a chance at being real Americans by forgetting the Chinese past?" (14). The latter question seems to project onto BaBa a role that is familiar in discourse about American immigrants and their children: that parents forsake or leave behind the native culture and language in order to accelerate the Americanization process of their offspring. Yet the text makes clear that BaBa's silence is not motivated by a desire on his part to ease his children's transition into American culture and society. He has not erased China in order to fill his children's lives with America; he's erased China and not presented his daughter any viable alternative to explain the family's origins. To his children, his silence on the subject of China and his past means that it does not exist. On her father's lack of words, the narrator declares, "You say with the few words and the silences: No stories. No past. No China" (14). Her seemingly anomalous statement—that her father can "say . . . silence"—demonstrates how silence can convey meaning, despite our cultural assumption that silence does not constitute a form of communication. In this case, the father's unwillingness to talk about China and his past seems to plunge both into an existence in which questions or answers are not possible.

But *China Men* doesn't end on this bleak note. As noted above, the final chapter has the narrator relishing her ability to listen to multiple stories; for once, she can hear a narrative, even if there are multiple versions of that narrative, rather than having to create it for herself from her father's silences and ellipses. A seemingly unrelated chapter near the end of *China Men* also seems to offer commentary on the possibilities of paternal silence. When the narrator's mother calls her brother, whom she hasn't seen in over fifty years, on New Year's Day, she bemoans the fact that even though it had been half a century since they last talked "we didn't say anything important." Her husband comforts her by telling her "That's the nature of phone calls. . . . You just hear each other's voices. That's enough" (220). BaBa's reassuring words to his wife also offer reassurance to his daughter: the narrator has been seeking to hear her father's experiences and history in order to know who he is, but as he says, perhaps just hearing the other person's voice—even if what he is saying isn't interesting or compelling or informative—is "enough."

CHAPTER 4

Tripmaster Monkey
His Fake Book

Kingston published *Tripmaster Monkey: His Fake Book,* her first and thus far only novel, in 1989. It has as its protagonist Wittman Ah Sing, a fifth-generation Chinese American living in San Francisco in the late 1960s, at the height of the countercultural and antiwar movements. Wittman is a recent Berkeley graduate, a hippie, an aspiring playwright, a reader, and a dreamer. He considers himself the twentieth-century reincarnation of the Monkey King (from the Chinese epic *Journey to the West*), and he is, in the words of Michiko Kakutani, a "compulsive teller of tales."[1] The novel follows Wittman as he meanders through San Francisco (with side excursions to Berkeley, Sacramento, and Reno), strategizing ways to avoid the draft, wooing and raging at various women, attending parties, visiting his parents and "aunties," and trying to collect unemployment benefits. *Tripmaster Monkey* ends with a performance of Wittman's play, which is acted by members of his family, his friends, acquaintances, and romantic interests—basically, everyone who has appeared in the novel. The novel's most salient feature is its episodic structure; indeed, much of the book consists of Wittman's monologues (spoken and internal) on a wide array of subjects pertaining to race, gender, sexuality, and nation and the stereotypes or assumptions associated with each of those identities.

The publication of as ambitious a novel as *Tripmaster Monkey* by as famous an author as Kingston was hotly anticipated. Profiles and interviews appeared in magazines, newspapers, and journals; with four books under her belt (*Hawai'i One Summer* had been released two years before *Tripmaster*) Kingston was well on her way to becoming one of the elder stateswomen of

American letters, with the honorary degrees, prestigious fellowships, and public lectures that such a position usually brings with it. The reviews for *Tripmaster* were favorable, with critics comparing Kingston to Gabriel García Márquez, Lenny Bruce, Salman Rushdie, and Allen Ginsberg.[2] Some readers expressed surprise that the protagonist of Kingston's first novel was a man; poet Marilyn Chin went so far as to ask Kingston "Why Wittman Ah Sing . . . and not Wilma Ah Lan? . . . I wasn't expecting a male protagonist."[3] As a writer who has always chafed against expectations and reveled in contradiction, it is not surprising that Kingston decided to make the lead character of her first novel a man rather than the woman many were anticipating. Indeed, in many ways, *Tripmaster Monkey* seems like a deliberate attempt to break with some of the figures and characters with which Kingston was most identified, even if her interest in certain themes and tropes remained as strong as ever. "Instead of the female avenger [of *The Woman Warrior*], we get Wittman," a Chinese American version of Huck Finn, Holden Caulfield, Augie March, Stephen Dedalus, and Abbie Hoffman.[4] In another unexpected move, through the years, it is Wittman that Kingston has returned to repeatedly, in works such as *The Fifth Book of Peace* and *I Love a Broad Margin to My Life;* he is clearly the character for whom she feels the most affinity and affection as she grows older.

Tripmaster Monkey differs in other ways from its literary predecessors. It shares with *China Men* and *The Woman Warrior* a disjointed and episodic form, but unlike those first two books, which jump through centuries or decades and in and out of different characters, the novel's action unfolds over the course of a few days. While John Leonard calls *The Woman Warrior* "a dream book" and *China Men* a "history lesson," he has trouble categorizing *Tripmaster Monkey* in such a pithy manner. *Tripmaster Monkey* does not give us the female avenger that *The Woman Warrior* taught us to expect, nor does it give us the history lessons that form the heart of *China Men*. Instead, it gives us Wittman, who "wants to be an authentic American, [only] America won't let him."[5] Wittman's verbal dramatics—both internal and spoken—lend *Tripmaster Monkey* what novelist Bharati Mukherjee calls its "brash, punchy, [and] loudmouthed" quality.[6] As Kakutani notes, Kingston's memoirs "were more or less tied together by familial connections" but Wittman's tales are "self-indulgent ego trips" that are strung together by whim.[7] These less than complimentary comments regarding Wittman's digressive personality permeate reader reactions to *Tripmaster.* Kingston admitted in an interview that most readers think Wittman has "an obnoxious personality," a quality which no doubt impacted their ability to identify with him in the same way that so many identified with the narrator in *The Woman Warrior.*[8] Mukherjee calls Wittman a "standup comic [who] goes for every joke, no matter how silly." Anne Tyler describes Wittman as the "23-year old [who has] taken up residence in our living room, staying way too long . . . and wearing us out with his exuberance."[9] Yet Wittman's relentless storytelling has a serious purpose: to tell the complex story of Chinese American culture and history and to convince everyone he meets that he and other Chinese Americans are an integral part of the United States. In his restless movements and his ceaseless talk, Wittman weaves together fantasies about Chinese America, critiques of racism, anxieties about romantic love, and his love of Chinese and Anglo-American literatures that effectively disrupt our expectations regarding the novel and what it means to be an American.

This chapter explores *Tripmaster Monkey: His Fake Book* as a text that consciously attempts to situate itself within both American and Chinese literary traditions and Wittman Ah Sing as an embodiment of a resistant Asian American political consciousness. *Tripmaster Monkey* revisits many of the themes and concerns raised in *The Woman Warrior* and *China Men* in terms of exploring the constitution of Chinese American identity, but its approach is much more overtly literary and identifiably postmodern, drawing upon and repurposing a wide array of cultural references, allusions, and histories from the West as well as from China. Whether quoting Rainer Maria Rilke, lambasting Frank Norris, or admiring *The Water Margin,* it is important to note that Kingston is revising the ideas behind these works, adapting them to fit her artistic notions, and infusing them with her own particular spin on their meanings.

Literary and Cultural References

Almost every critic and reviewer of *Tripmaster Monkey* notes its incorporation of an ecumenical range of cultural references. From these "bits and pieces of assorted mainstream cultures," Kingston has assembled a novel about a Chinese American hippie playwright living in San Francisco.[10] According to Jonna Mackin, what makes the novel comical is the "unexpected juxtaposition of culturally unlike elements."[11] This joining up of disparate components does more than elicit appreciative laughter from the reader; it also highlights how identity emerges from the complex, hybridic, and ever-shifting interplay between a variety of cultural histories and elements, many of them often unexpected. To start with the most obvious example, Wittman Ah Sing's name clearly invokes the American poet Walt Whitman; indeed, we are told that Wittman's father deliberately named his son after the poet. "'My name is Wittman Ah Sing, but you may call me Bold'" Wittman self-assuredly and grandly declares early in the novel in response to a request by Nanci Lee, a fellow Berkeley alum and aspiring actress, that he read her some of his poetry.[12] His confident rhetoric, the way he proclaims his name and asserts his vitality to the audience is highly reminiscent of the opening line of Whitman's most famous poem "Song of Myself": "I celebrate myself, and sing myself."

That Kingston pays homage to the most American of all poets should not be surprising. In bearing Walt Whitman's name, Wittman claims the ability to embody the ideals of the nation, to be the symbol of American democracy and artistic expression, an insistence on Chinese American belonging that one can find throughout her works. Wittman announces that "his province is America; America, his province" (41). More than anything, Wittman is determined to claim America as his—and by extension, the Chinese American community's—own. When he speaks of America, he is speaking of himself and vice versa. At the end of the novel, as he delivers his monologue following the performance of his play, Wittman goes on to state that "we have eyes that won the West" (314), a play perhaps on the stereotype that Asians have "slant" eyes or another stereotype that "Asian culture" subordinates the individual (the "I") to the community. (Or as Irma Maini argues, "by declaring his eyes American, Wittman is clearly validating a physical feature of Asian Americans that has been subject to countless racist jokes and stereotypes."[13]) Wittman's monologue is another revision of Chinese American history, as he tells his audience that for "a moment a hundred years ago, we were China Men. After all, the other people in the new world were Englishmen and Frenchmen and Dutchmen. But they changed themselves into Americans, and wouldn't let us change into Americans. And they slurred 'China Man.' 'Chinaman,' they said dactylically" (326). Wittman's etymology of the word "Chinaman" suggests that there was a moment in American history—before it really was America—when Chinese men were just like the other men who were in the "new world." The transformation of "China Man" into "Chinaman" reflects the racialization process that the Chinese underwent after these early years. But for Wittman, the insult still retains the roots of that democratic and inclusive potential.

Walt Whitman is not just present in the protagonist's name. "Whitmanian content" abounds throughout *Tripmaster Monkey.*[14] Kingston nods to Walt Whitman again when she reveals that Wittman's Chinese name is "Joang Fu" (37), which means "Inner Truth." Several chapter titles in *Tripmaster Monkey* directly reference titles from Whitman's *Leaves of Grass:* "Trippers and Askers" is taken from "Song of Myself" while Whitman's poems "Song of the Open Road" and "A Song for Occupations" are both cited multiple times in the novel. As Tanner argues, the "significance of Kingston's use of this title is simply to indicate that Wittman's focus "is not on the life of the external world but the interior life of the imagination."[15] It is important to note, however, these citations are never "straight," and Kingston never makes an easy comparison between her Wittman and Whitman the poet. As Tanner points out, Walt

Whitman's "A Song for Occupations" is a celebration of the possibilities of independent labor, in which Whitman's expansive narrator becomes, in the words of Alan Trachtenberg, the "great poet" of laissez-faire economics.[16] "A Song for Occupations" in *Tripmaster Monkey* depicts a very different scene from that in the poem. The chapter recounts Wittman's attempts to maneuver through hostile and byzantine state bureaucracies in order to receive his unemployment benefits. In this attempt, he is guided by an elderly Asian American woman, who tells him how to answer the questions of the unemployment officer and even gives him a cheat sheet. This interaction subtly evokes a different kind of history than that which Walt Whitman represents: the Chinese "paper sons" who attempted to enter America by claiming fathers and families that were not their own. The cheat sheet that Wittman receives from the Chinese lady at the unemployment office is a twentieth-century version of the cheat sheets that paper sons studied in order to enter the United States. The office warns benefits seekers not to bring relatives or friends to their interviews, another example in Wittman's mind of how entry into the United States requires the immigrant to forsake all ties to his or her communities. Despite the requirement that interviewees be "alienated, tribeless" (246), Chinese Americans find a way to form community, even if it is momentary or contingent.

Thus, Walt Whitman is not the guiding spirit of *Tripmaster Monkey* so much as the embodiment of all that America seems to offer but never actually proffers to Chinese American men. Cyrus Patell notes that in invoking Walt Whitman, Kingston is both "tipping her hat to the great poet of American individualism and gently mocking him. Kingston's novel depicts a young poet-playwright who wants to be another Whitman—a Great American Artist—but finds that first he must disengage himself from the subordinate place that US culture has made for him on the basis of his ethnicity."[17] In other words, while *Tripmaster Monkey* celebrates Walt Whitman's place as Great American Poet, it also gently questions whether that preeminent position in the American cultural and literary canon is not the result of his racial and gender privilege. These references to Walt Whitman throughout *Tripmaster Monkey* suggest an agonized relationship between Chinese Americans and poetic expression—that given the erasure of Chinese Americans historically and the materially difficult conditions under which they lived for decades, there can be no Chinese American Whitman.

Whitman is by no means the only figure that *Tripmaster Monkey* alludes to in its depiction of Wittman's progression toward Chinese American artist. During the course of *Tripmaster Monkey,* Wittman also mentions James Joyce, Beats, Rainer Maria Rilke (whose work *The Notebooks of Malte Laurids Brigge* he reads aloud on buses for the other passengers' enjoyment), *West Side*

Story, jazz music, and the Beatniks, to name a few. Jazz in particular offers another model for thinking about the novel's formal structure. The subtitle of *Tripmaster Monkey—His Fake Book*—is borrowed from the jazz world. As defined by Kingston, a "fake book" is a compilation "of basic tunes, songs, and chords. Sometimes it would be just the beginning of a tune, then [jazz musicians] would improvise. So I was trying to write a prose book with a basic plot, suggestions for social action, for trips. I hope to trip the reader out and have them improvise further."[18] Combining jazz with a counter-cultural figure like a trip master (ostensibly, one who "guides" drug users while they are under the influence of mind-altering substances) situates *Tripmaster Monkey* the novel within a particular antiestablishment tradition. In describing *Tripmaster* as essentially a series of sketches that depends upon the reader's engagement with the material, Kingston is clearly trying to redefine the novel structurally and politically. In comparing her book to a jazz fake book, Kingston is not positioning her readers as the listeners but rather as the musicians; in other words, they are not passively receiving the themes and ideas the book explores but are active participants in creating their own communities. Presenting *Tripmaster* as a fake book, Kingston puts the onus back on her readers for creating their own artistic endeavors and social action. *Tripmaster* then is the first song in an otherwise long set of potential community-building endeavors. It is this notion of community building that appears repeatedly throughout the novel: Whitman is not merely trying to find his community or run from his community, he is looking to build a different, more inclusive type of community.

While jazz offers a useful framework for thinking about community creation and involvement, Kingston also decouples it from the particular history of its production and dissemination. In other words, Kingston is looking to an African American cultural history to provide a structure and vocabulary for conceptualizing Asian American artistic endeavors without acknowledging the historical conditions that produced that art in the first place. This cultural borrowing is expressly articulated in the novel by Wittman, who asks "Where's our jazz? Where's our blues? Where's our ain't-taking-no-shit-from-nobody street-strutting language? I want so bad to be the first bad-jazz China Man bluesman of America" (27). Jazz and the blues stand in Wittman's mind as the standard for antiracist, subversive cultural practices, and his assertion that Asian Americans do not have the same kind of rich linguistic and cultural tools to combat anti-Asian racism echoes the lamentations of many Asian American cultural nationalists of the 1970s who looked to African American subjects and history as models for resistance. But Wittman's petulant demand for a "China Man bluesman of America" ignores the fact that jazz emerged in African American culture under a set of circumstances that were very different from what Chinese Americans endured. This is also a moment that Mackin points to when she argues that Kingston's playful use of pastiche "veils contradictions . . . that are problematic for a self-proclaimed pacifist communitarian."[19] Because Kingston doesn't specifically name African American jazz performers anywhere in the novel nor in her interview explaining the origins of the fake book, Mackin suggests that African Americans are "the third party in *Tripmaster Monkey*."[20] Mackin particularly critiques the "performance of racial identity" in the novel, suggesting that its parodic representations of both Chinese American and African American identities conceals a hostility toward the political activism of antiracism campaigns of the 1960s and beyond. Mackin's critique suggests that Kingston uses black characters as a metaphor for racial exclusion and injustice, evacuating that community's history of its material, physical, and economic particularities in the service of exploring Chinese American subjectivity.

The other centrally important inspirations and source texts for *Tripmaster Monkey* are from the Chinese classical tradition: *Journey to the West* (attributed to Wu Cheng'en, c. early 17th century), *Three Kingdoms* (attributed to Luo Guanzhong, c. fourteenth century), and *The Water Margin* (attributed to Shi Nai'an, c. fourteenth century). Patricia Chu argues that Chinese myths are a "rich but open-ended source of inspiration for [Kingston's] Chinese American cultural creation[s]";[21] in particular, she calls *Journey to the West* the "touchstone" text of *Tripmaster Monkey*, because unlike the other Chinese classical texts, it does not concern itself with war but rather with the retrieval of sacred texts.[22] Wittman at multiple points in the novel cloaks himself in the mantle of the Monkey King, Sun Wu Kong, perhaps because he is capable of seventy-two physical transformations. Sun Wu Kong is the most famous member of a group of pilgrims charged with bringing back to China the Buddhist sutras. *Journey to the West* depicts the Monkey as cunning, powerful, and childlike in his behavior, qualities that have led many to call him a trickster figure and that would obviously be appealing to someone like Wittman, who is seeking out models for his own Chinese American identity. Kingston's version of *Journey to the West* has the pilgrims discovering that the scrolls they have been given are blank; outraged, they demand an exchange and receive a set of scrolls with words. But the narrator of *Tripmaster Monkey* concludes that "the empty scrolls had been the right ones all along" (42). For Chu, Kingston's iteration of this tale highlights Kingston's "preference for a Chinese tradition whose greatest worth comes from its refusal of texts as authorities."[23] *Journey to the West* denies the power of text, thereby encouraging its own reinscription into various contexts and forms.

Wittman also narrates a highly compressed version of the *Three Kingdoms* to Taña de Weese soon after they are married. In Wittman's telling, Lady Sun marries the general Liu Bei although they are from rival political factions. Despite the fact that they are happily married, Liu constantly fears that his wife will betray him in order to help the cause of her brother who also happens to be Liu's enemy. Only when she saves her husband's life as they are fleeing her family's advancing army does he fully realize how resourceful and brave she is. As Chu points out, Wittman's version of the story is quite different from the original version of *Three Kingdoms.* Wittman's retelling grants agency and voice to Lady Sun, who in the original version is merely a pawn in the political and military struggles between her brother Sun Quan and her husband Liu Bei. According to Chu, "though Lady Sun is supposedly the most important woman in *Three Kingdoms,* she has no part in the action once [the] wedding" takes place.[24] The relationships at the heart of the original novel are the rivalry between Liu and Sun as well as the deep friendship and camaraderie between Liu and his principal advisor Zhuge Liange. In the original story, it is Zhuge who saves Liu's life time and again, Zhuge who is the most loyal friend, Zhuge whom Liu cries for on his own deathbed. Chu reads Kingston's feminist revision of this Chinese tale as necessarily incomplete, because the "story's patriarchal assumptions are too deeply embedded in its plot" and in its representation of the characters.[25] In other words, Kingston can only revise not radicalize this story. Kingston's emphasis on the equity between Lady Sun and her husband and romantic love between the two characters does nothing to alter the fact that *Three Kingdoms* views women as fundamentally untrustworthy—in the case of Lady Sun, she will either betray her brother or betray her husband. The fact that Kingston's version is told by Wittman to his new wife Taña is also telling and seems to undermine the feminist potential of Kingston's revision. A story of perfect wifely loyalty as much as it is a tale of heterosexual romantic marriage, it seems a commentary on the role that Taña will play in the novel. Although she is a feminist, an artist, and constantly surprises Wittman with the depth of her compassion and understanding regarding racial issues, she does not have an independent presence outside of her husband. She is, in fact, a modern version of Lady Sun, offering to marry Wittman to save him from the draft and then proving to be a loyal and patient wife even when he is at his most difficult and moody.

Finally, Wittman describes the play he is writing as a revision of the Chinese classic *The Water Margin.* Kingston transforms the story of 108 bandits who form their own army and are eventually sent out by the imperial government to fight foreign invaders into an encyclopedic multifaceted narrative of Chinese American experiences. Kingston suggests that the identity that Chinese Americans should embrace in order to counter accounts of the Yellow Peril or the Model Minority is that of bandit and rebel. Wittman dares the sheriff who comes to the Benevolent Association during his play's run to complain about the noise to arrest the entire troupe of actors, whom he calls "more than 108 outlaws" (302). In taunting law enforcement, Wittman proclaims a new version of Asian American history, one that transforms figures that have traditionally been marginalized, excluded, and victimized—the wildcat miners, the aliens ineligible for citizenship, the gamblers, the draft dodgers, the Communists, the "japs and Viet Cong"—into bandits and rebels. According to Jeanne Rosier Smith, Kingston sets forth the notion that the "secret to a strong Chinese American community . . . lies in this redefinition of Chinese Americans as outlaws."[26]

Kingston revises these Chinese myths not to mislead readers about China but to highlight the *process* through which Chinese America is formed and constructed. Monkeying with the myths in such a self-conscious manner highlights the fact that Chinese Americans *must* adapt and alter their understanding of Chinese culture in order to survive and thrive in the United States. As a writer who has stated publicly in interviews that she is "proud of being convoluted" and that "I try to be convoluted," it is perhaps easy to label Kingston's presentation of Chinese myth and legend in *Tripmaster Monkey* as an example of an author changing source material simply for the sake of creating confusion, discord, or chaos.[27] However, it isn't just that Kingston enjoys ambiguity and difficulty in her writing (although she does), it is that she is working to frustrate any attempts on the part of readers to "totalize and anthropologize" her work to apply to Chinese or Chinese Americans.[28] It is not just that she is celebrating revision for revision's sake—she is "affirm[ing] the authority of individual readers, interpretive communities, and contemporary authors to engage dialogically" with cultural traditions and texts. As Kingston herself notes in talking about *China Men,* if her father—who is the source for her narrative—has the right to tell multiple versions of stories about his arrival in America, then she—as the writer—has the same right.

Postmodern Wittman

Kingston's belief that stories can exist in multiple versions and that they are made and remade by readers and listeners as much as they are by authors and speakers articulates one of the premises of the postmodern novel, with which *Tripmaster Monkey* is often identified. E. D. Huntley argues that *Tripmaster Monkey* has more in common with James Joyce's *Ulysses* or *Finnegans Wake* than it does with most Asian American literature, because it embraces a narrative structure that is "fractured, disjointed, chaotic" and even "unfathomable and opaque" to many readers.[29] Hsiao-Hung Chang calls the novel "an imaginary space of heteroglossia," while John Leonard focuses on the novel's language, stating that it "bounces, caroms and collides; abrades and inflames."[30] While most critics focus on the novel's form or its narrator's exuberant rhetoric in order to make the case for its postmodern label, Linda Hutcheon takes a slightly different tack; she argues that what makes Kingston's novel postmodern is the "presence of the past."[31] Hutcheon asserts that postmodernist work takes a critical stance toward the past, engages with it in "an ironic dialogue . . . a recalling of a critically shared vocabulary. . . . Its aesthetic forms and its social formations are problematized by critical reflection. . . . It is always a critical reworking, never a nostalgic 'return.'"[32] In countering critics such as Frederic Jameson who condemn what they see as postmodernism's ahistoricity and its uncritical relationship to late capitalist systems, Hutcheon famously makes the case that postmodernism is "fundamentally contradictory, resolutely historical, and inescapably political."[33] She also argues that postmodernism "takes the form of self-conscious, self-contradictory, self-undermining statement."[34] For Hutcheon, Kingston is firmly within the postmodernist canon not only because of the form her works take but also because of her unflinching critiques of racism, sexism, war, nationalism, and violence.

Nowhere is that more apparent than in the novel's exploration of Chinese America, particularly the tension between the individual subject and the ethnic community with which he or she identifies. Wittman's ambivalence toward his ancestry and the way that it circulates in the US context is reflected in the novel's narrative voice, which is not in the first person, as one might have expected based on Kingston's previous works. Instead, *Tripmaster Monkey* has an omniscient third-person narrative voice, who "often makes herself visible as both observer and participant in narrated action."[35] This destabilizing of the distinction between self and community, between narrator and character reflects the novel's conception of race and identity as process. Near the novel's end, the narrator describes Wittman's monologue following the staging of his play as an attempt at "defining a community." The narrator then acknowledges that "we're going to reward and bless Wittman with listening while he talks to his heart's content. Let him get it all out, and we hear what he has to say direct" (306). Here, the narrator acts almost like a chorus in a Greek play: an integral part of the work that represents the community and comments on the actions of the participants. This communal narrator respects Wittman's perspective, even as it mocks him at times, and considers him a part of the Chinese American community even when Wittman seems to reject that affiliation: "Our monkey, master of change, staged a fake war, which might very well be displacing some real war. Wittman was learning that one big-bang show has to be followed up with a second show, a third show, shows until something take hold. He was defining a community, which will meet every night for a season. Community is not built once and for all; people have to imagine, practice, and re-create it" (306). This passage highlights Kingston's view that identity and community are works-in-progress: they must constantly be redefined and altered in order to remain vibrant and relevant. Debra Shostak calls Kingston's narrative voice in these instances "transpersonal or communal," a characterization that I find useful as it recognizes the existence of a present and vibrant Chinese American collectivity that welcomes and resists Wittman.[36]

The novel's narrative voice emphasizes the contradictory and constructed nature of subjectivity, but it is Wittman himself who grapples with these questions especially as he attempts to write his play. In describing the creative process for a writer of color, Kingston suggests that Wittman's play is an attempt to write himself into an identity that he cannot otherwise articulate: "And again whammed into the block question: Does he announce now that the author is—Chinese? Or rather, Chinese-American? And be forced into autobiographical confession. Stop the music—I have to butt in and introduce myself and my race" (34). Wittman's struggle about when to interject his ethnic identity into the play also raises questions about what it means to be Chinese American artist. For in raising the issue of his race, is he not simply acceding to the demands of a reading public who want ethnic authors to authenticate themselves, who want their narratives to be a form of "autobiographical confession"? This is the question that all Chinese American authors—and to a broader extent, all ethnic American authors—confront, and it is a question, as Kingston has noted in other works, that has the potential to block the creative process altogether. The internal conflict that he repeatedly confronts reflects Hutcheon's point that the postmodern novel is deeply invested in questions of history and of politics, just as our constructions of race, gender, and other identity markers are formed and then influence our perceptions of history, nation, and citizenship.

For Wittman, writing represents an attempt to construct a Chinese American self and simultaneously resist the racist representations of the Chinese that he confronts and has internalized. And in fact, the easiest way to describe *Tripmaster Monkey* might be to call it a book about the process of writing. It is, in other words, a novel that is singularly obsessed with the process of narration. As Wittman attempts to write his play one night, he is plagued by the sound of a neighbor "tapping, tapping at a typewriter, a typing through the night." Even though Wittman desperately wants to imagine that this typing sound is something mechanical and nonintentional—a furnace, a teletype, a timer—he knows that

> an intelligence was coming up with words. Someone else, not a poet with pencil or fountain pen but a workhorse big-novel writer, was staying up, probably done composing already and typing out fair copy. It should be a companionable noise, a jazz challenge to which he could blow out the window his answering jazz. But, no, it's an expensive electric machine-gun typewriter aiming at him, gunning for him, to knock him off in competition. But so efficient—it had to be a girl, a clerk typist, he hoped, a secretary he hoped. A schoolteacher cutting mimeo stencils. A cookbook writer. A guidebook-for-tourists writer. Madam Dim Sum, Madam Chinoiserie, Madam Orientalia knocking out horsey cocky locky astrology, Horatio Algiers Wong—he heard the typing leave him behind. (41)

Patricia Chu reads this scene of Wittman "haunted by the tapping of a rival's typewriter," as an allusion to Frank Chin and Kingston's response to the hostility that Chin has evinced over the years to more successful and acclaimed Asian American authors like Kingston.[37] But to cite this passage as an artistic rendering of the Chinese American pen wars does not acknowledge the complexity of artistic creation and therefore subjective formation. Here, Wittman expresses envy over the productivity of the writer who shares his wall and hopes that he or she is a typist merely transcribing someone else's words or producing schlock, popular books (cookbooks, travel books). He also conjectures that the reason that the typing is happening so efficiently is because the writer is relying upon stereotypes to churn out pages. That is the only way he can imagine a Chinese American writer typing so quickly: that he or she is drawing upon a deep and well established tradition of orientalist representation.

The passage also emphasizes the materiality of what it takes to put words down on paper as well as a description of what it feels like to not be able to write. It is a passage, in other words, that encapsulates writing and nonwriting, passivity and creativity and the agony that can be associated with both states of mind. It is the novel's emphasis on Wittman's writing process that leads critics to call *Tripmaster Monkey* a *Künstlerroman*: a narrative that "highlights the marginality of the artist . . . at odds with a hostile world. More often than not, it is the artist's unique artistic and intellectual sensibility that leads to this alienation from society."[38] Wittman's obsession with the source of this typing also reflects the fact that identity does not happen in an artistic or social vacuum. He worries that the typing is "leav[ing] him behind," a sign, in other words, that he is losing time that he can never recover or a sign that he will never be able to get the words he wants to articulate out of his head and onto paper. Wittman evaluates his progress as a writer, just as he evaluates his own sense of his identity, in relation to those around him.

Who Is Wittman?

Burdened as he is with all of these inconsistent impulses, Wittman struggles with how to articulate himself as an individual given the stereotypes and assumptions associated with his community. The question he plaintively poses at his friend Lance's party—"How do you reconcile unity and identity?" (105)—echoes a question that Kingston asked in *The Woman Warrior:* "What's Chinese tradition and what's the movies?" (6). Both of these questions are ultimately about what it means to be Chinese American in a country that considers Asians to be forever foreign. How can an individual Chinese American subject express him or herself given the long-standing racist discourse that informs how the community as a whole is perceived? Given how pervasive that history is and how inescapable, what part—if any—of a Chinese American subject can be formed outside of that racist history? How does one identify with a community that has been so vilified discursively, politically, and physically and retain a sense of self?

These are questions without easy answers. Early in the novel, Wittman asks Nanci, "If the Chinese American culture is not knickknackatory—look at it—backscratcher swizzle sticks, pointed chopsticks for the hair, Jade East aftershave in a Buddha shaped bottle, the head screws off and you pour lotion out of its neck—then what is it? . . . So what do we have in the way of Chinese culture besides Chinese hand laundries?" (27). Here Wittman expresses an anxiety that Chinese American culture is nothing more than an oriental bazaar, that it contains nothing other than the commodified products of anti-Chinese racism. It is this fear—that Chinese American culture has come to be defined by an orientalist discourse even for Chinese Americans themselves—that informs Wittman's urgent desire to create an antiracist and resistant Chinese American identity.

Wittman himself is constantly and painfully aware of how others perceive him as a Chinese American man. When he meets new people, he braces himself for the moment when they will say something ignorant or racist about the Chinese. In many ways, his hyperconsciousness about racism defines him more thoroughly than anything else. It is this hyperawareness that leads to defensiveness, and it is this defensiveness (as in the incident with Nanci) that other characters (and readers) tend to find alienating and immature. For example, while driving his car Wittman focuses all of his concentration "on counteracting his stereotype. If he were Black, no Cadillac; if he were Mexican American, no duck ass on his head, and no 'fifty Merc, raked and deshocked, waddling through the downtown; if he were a girl, no red Mustang; if he were a socialist, no V.W. with a Co-op bumpersticker" (208). So aware is Wittman of the stereotypes associated with race, so eager is he to avoid fitting into these stereotypes, that every choice he has to make or every situation in which he finds himself—no matter now mundane or trivial—elicits an excruciating calculus for determining how he should respond or behave. His method for dealing with this sense of surveillance and scrutiny is to cultivate a hypermasculine, disruptive, nonconformist persona that nevertheless cannot quite hide the insecurities and anxieties that he feels. Jennie Wang calls Wittman a "Postmodern representation of a new 'China Man,' who redefines the national character of an American," but it is important to note that this "new China Man" is very much aware of the lingering and powerful presence of the "old" China Man."[39] Wittman's attempts to fashion a new Chinese American identity is just as much about destroying that stereotype as it is about staking out any kind of new identity position for Chinese American masculinity. In this sense Wittman's "new China Man" can be corrective—which is important in a country in which historical erasures and stereotypes abound so frequently—but cannot be revolutionary. In other words, he is so obsessed with combatting stereotypes about Chinese American men that he finds it difficult to articulate a new vision of Chinese American identity that isn't reacting to what came before.

One of the ways that Wittman and many other Asian nationalists of the 1960s and 1970s resisted white racism was by aligning themselves with and adopting the rhetoric of the Black Nationalist movement. For example, when Nanci tells Wittman "You sound black. . . . I mean like a Black poet. Jive. Slang. Like LeRoi Jones. Like . . . like Black," Wittman loses his temper and reacts aggressively: "He slammed his hand—fist with a poem in it—down on the desk—fistful of poem. He spit in his genuine brass China Man spittoon, and jumped on top of the desk, squatted there, scratching. 'Monkey see, monkey do?' he said. 'Huh? Monkey see, monkey do?' Which sounds much uglier if you know Chinese. 'Monkey shit, monkey belly.' 'A lot you know,' he said, 'A lot you know about us monkeys.' She got up and stood behind her chair. He sprang from the desk onto the chair, and from the chair to the mattress and from the mattress up onto the desk again, dragging his long arms and heavy knuckles" (32). The monkey that Wittman invokes has multiple layers of meaning. Wittman is clearly performing the Monkey King from the Chinese epic *Journey to the* West. The monkey as trickster also calls to mind the signifying monkey of African American culture. In both Chinese and African American cultures, the monkey is a figure for ingenuity and resistance. It is, however, this link between Chinese and African American culture that also triggers Wittman's anger, for Nanci's comment that Wittman's poetic voice "sound[s] black" taps into Wittman's fear that his work will seem derivative or an echo of the resistant voices that precede him. Wittman wants to be a new kind of China Man, but the only resistant language he can access is what Jonna Mackin calls "recycled speech," that is, black speech. What Wittman fears is that there is nothing resistant about Asian American linguistic conventions and that whatever he creates will be seen as nothing more than repetition of what has already been said. Wittman's anger at Nanci's inability to appreciate his attempts to forge new kinds of models for Chinese Americans reflects the insecurity with which he constantly struggles.

It is altogether fitting therefore, given Wittman's interest in performance, that the novel ends with a piece of theater and Wittman's diatribe on the audience's reaction to it. Like the Monkey King, who brought Buddhism to China from India, Wittman decides to bring China to America through his play, which will be filled with figures from Chinese classics, showgirls, Chang and Eng Bunker, Edith and Winnifred Eaton, fireworks, fistfights, Frank Norris, and Chinese American history. Wittman imagines a stage in which the curtain is made out of tinsel, and "lights with blue gels will shaft through the very dark house and play on the moving rain-fringe curtains, which represent a waterfall. I want to suggest mermaids and flashing salmon, fluke tails flipping in the sun, sequins of water, Lorelei sequins, rainbows and trout refracting and multiplying" (134). He also imagines disco lights, mirror balls, and a week-long production, in which the "audience comes back every night for the continuation. They live with us [the actors]" (149). Much like the novel itself, Wittman's play is a collage of forms and genres, a mixture of found objects and epic fantasies.

In order to reconcile the seemingly competing claims made of the ethnic author to represent one's culture in a nonstereotypical, nonorientalist manner and reflect her own "individual artistic vision" all while working with material that has historically been deemed unworthy of memory or history, Kingston turns in *Tripmaster Monkey* to a notion of performativity that "resists the opposition of fact and imagination."[40] Wittman's play nods to history even as it mocks the foundations of that narrative mode. When Wittman cheekily quotes that "the play's the thing," he is really speaking of a fundamental tenet of the novel. Wittman's play makes clear the role that race can play in the production of authorship and the literary process: "This play is immense. Epic. Our story won't fit a one-act on a unit set of crates and burlap bags. I'm going to bring back to theater the long and continuous play that goes on for a week without repeating itself. Because life is long and continuous. The way theater was in the old days. I mean the old days in this country. The audience comes back every night for the continuation. They live with us" (149). This image of an ongoing performance that blurs theater with real life leads Jonna Mackin to argue that performativity lies at center of the novel, and that it represents Kingston's solution to her "difficult quest to combine individual creativity with cultural authenticity."[41] Lara Narcisi makes the same case when she states that *Tripmaster Monkey* represents the "valorization of performance."[42] Sun Hee Teresa Lee argues that performance "allows Kingston to articulate an empowered subject position" that cannot otherwise be attained through language and narrative, precisely because the written word for the ethnic author carries with it a particular set of burdens: the desire on the part of readers for a Chinese other who is an "authentic" symbol.[43] Wittman's vision for his play is one in which performance blends into the everyday and becomes indistinguishable from it—actors and audience become one.

Wittman's play is a pastiche, a composite of multiple genres that contains melodrama, epic, monologue, satire, and history. Wittman's mingling of stories and histories echoes Kingston's manipulation and reconfiguration of the novel's genre, and both echo the process by which Chinese American identity is constructed: if Chinese American identity is a kind of genre of identity, with rules and foundations, then Kingston is interested in reinventing both. The long monologue that Wittman addresses to his audience at the conclusion of his play elucidates and describes that reinvention. Having directed and staged his play—which enacts his vision of the inconsistencies and paradoxes that constitute Chinese American experience—he comes onstage after the final performance to explain that all of the viewers—even the Chinese American ones—have interpreted it incorrectly. According to Mita Banerjee, the fact that Wittman comes out to explain his point once he realizes that viewers may not be "getting" it reflects the tension within *Tripmaster Monkey* between what Banerjee calls the "aesthetic" and the "didactic."[44] There is a similar tension at play in Wittman's earlier question about the relationship between unity and individuality; Wittman uses aesthetic forms and tropes in order to deconstruct orientalist stereotypes regarding the Chinese, but because he does not fully believe that society has moved beyond these stereotypes, he feels compelled to explain his aesthetic choices to audiences in order to point to where the critique is.

He first rails against the very title of "Chinese American" to identify the community: "When I hear you call yourselves 'Chinese,' I take you to mean American-understood, but too lazy to say it. You do mean 'Chinese' as short for 'Chinese-American,' don't you? We mustn't call ourselves 'Chinese' among those who are ready to send us back to where they think we came from. But 'Chinese-American' takes too long. Nobody says or hears past the first part. And 'Chinese-American' is inaccurate—as if we could have two countries. We need to take the hyphen out—'Chinese Americans.' However. Not okay yet. 'Chinese hyphen American' sounds exactly the same as 'Chinese no hyphen American.' No revolution takes place in the mouth or in the ear" (327). The notion that nobody listens past the first word in the phrase "Chinese-American" suggests that nobody *wants* to hear the second word in that phrase. As Wittman notes, Chinese Americans shouldn't emphasize the first part of their identity when they're in the midst of people who want to "send us back where they think we came from." The hyphen that Wittman rails against is embodied in his play by the conjoined/separate figures of Chang and Eng, "the double boys," who can only be identified as (t)he(y): "'We know damned well what you came for to see—the angle we're joined at, how we can have two sisters for wives and twenty-one Chinese Carolinian children between us. You want to see if there's room for two, three bundling boards. You want to know if we feel jointly. You want to look at the hyphen. You want to look at it bare'" (293). Isabella Furth calls the hyphen, "the mark that simultaneously conjoins and separates" two things, a particularly vexing signal to racial minorities in the United States: valorizing the hyphen may unwittingly reinforce orientalist discourses regarding the differences between "East" and "West" while ignoring it, or letting the hyphen drop away, allows for the erasure of a certain kind of racial history and practice.

Other kinds of racial practices remain as strong as ever, much to Wittman's chagrin. The critical response to Wittman's play—while positive overall—enrages him.

> "Let me discuss with you what the *Chron* and the *Examiner* said, and the *Oakland Tribune* and *The Daily Cal* and the *Berkeley Gazette,* and the *Shopping News,* and the *Barb.* They've reviewed us already, thinking that opening night is no different from the second night and tonight. You like the reviews? I'm sore and disappointed. Come on, you can't like these reviews. Don't be too easily made happy. Look. Look. 'East meets West.' 'Exotic.' 'Sino-American theater.' 'Snaps, crackles and pops like singing rice.' 'Sweet and sour.' Quit clapping. Stop it. What's there to cheer about? You like being compared to Rice Krispies? Cut it out. Let me show you, you've been insulted. They sent their food critics. They wrote us up like they were tasting Chinese food. Rice, get it? 'Savor beauteous Nanci Lee,' it says here. That's like saying that LeRoi Jones is as good as a watermelon. 'Yum yum, authentic watermelon.' They wouldn't write a headline for *Raisin in the Sun:* 'America Meets Africa.' They want us to go back to China where we belong." (307)

Wittman's diatribe against the critics—even the ones who enjoyed and praised the play—cannot help but echo his creator's reaction to some of the reviewers of *The Woman Warrior.* Critics enjoyed *The Woman Warrior* because they thought it offered a window into the mysteries of China, even though the narrator has never been to China and her descriptions of China are based on her mother's stories. The comparison of Chinese American culture to Chinese food suggests the reductive way in which the former is viewed: as something easily consumable and commodifiable that exists to be enjoyed by white Americans. Wittman insists the way that the play is written about by critics betrays a subtle hostility towards the Chinese in the United States, one that wishes to see the Chinese as forever foreign because that would mean that they would one day have to go back "where [they] belong."

The Wittman at the novel's end is very different from the one we met at the start of the novel. *Tripmaster Monkey* begins with Wittman cursing the "FOBs" he runs across in his walk across Golden Gate Park, the Chinese in America who seem to validate all of the stereotypes about Asians that Wittman hates and rails against. By the end of the book, he expresses a more conciliatory—though still acerbic—attitude toward his own ancestry and community. The novel ends on a note of detente if not reconciliation: "Wittman's community was blessing him, whether he liked it or not" (340). The relationship between Wittman and his "community" is not a full-on reconciliation—the pains and traumas of Wittman's childhood and the history of Chinese exclusion run too deeply perhaps for that. But the community's acceptance of his play and himself indicates that there is a kind of bond between the two, regardless of Wittman's ambivalence or resentment.

The sense that the community at least welcomes Wittman even if he isn't so sure how he feels is further emphasized in the novel's final line: "Studying the mightiest war epic of all time, Wittman changed—bee-e-en!—into a pacifist. Dear American monkey, don't be afraid. Here, let us tweak your ear, and kiss your other ear" (340). Wittman's transformation from angry young man to pacifist is not as complete as the narrative suggests at the end; that would entail a sense of closure that the character himself never can never fully embody or articulate. However, the narrator's assumption of a communal Chinese American identity highlights the welcome that this community offers an "American monkey" like Wittman. The narrator acknowledges Wittman's attempt to embody the American monkey and supports it, even as she gently mocks him for it at the same time.

CHAPTER 5

Hawai'i One Summer, The Fifth Book of Peace, and *Veterans of War, Veterans of Peace*

Kingston's reputation as a bestselling and distinguished author rests primarily on *The Woman Warrior, China Men,* and *Tripmaster Monkey: His Fake Book.* She has, however, published four additional books in addition to these classics: *To Be the Poet* (2002) and *I Love a Broad Margin to My Life* (2011), both volumes of poetry; *The Fifth Book of Peace* (2003), a memoir with long sections of prose fiction; and *Hawai'i One Summer, 1978* (1987; hereafter *Hawai'i One Summer*), a collection of essays about her life in that state. Since the 1980s, Kingston has also been organizing and running writing workshops for Vietnam War veterans primarily in California, and in 2006, a selection of these pieces by veterans were published as *Veterans of War, Veterans of Peace* (2006) with Kingston serving as the volume's editor and writing a brief introduction.[1] The subject of this chapter will be the prose works mentioned above—*Hawai'i One Summer, The Fifth Book of Peace,* and more briefly, her work for and in *Veterans of War, Veterans of Peace*—and the ways in which they fit into the themes and concerns of Kingston's previous, more famous works and at the same time represent a shift in priorities both politically and aesthetically. All three of these texts continue to explore some of Kingston's long-held interests in issues of racial identity as well as the often fraught relationship between and individual and his or her community. Additionally, *The Fifth Book of Peace* and, to a lesser extent, *Hawai'i One Summer,* demonstrate the continuing importance of Wittman Ah Sing to Kingston's literary project. *The Fifth Book of Peace* contains a long section focusing on the Ah Sings and their move to Hawai'i, a journey that clearly is patterned after Kingston's own experiences moving to and living in that state as narrated in *Hawai'i One Summer.* These two volumes highlight the extent to which Wittman has become a kind of literary alter ego to Kingston, a development that is slightly surprising given the fact that Wittman is so often discussed in the critical literature—in far too simplistic or literal ways, in my opinion—as a stand-in for Frank Chin. Wittman's reappearance in these texts signals the extent to which Kingston finds him a useful figure for exploring a variety of issues, race and gender being two of the most important, but also aging, family life, and socioeconomic difficulties.

It is also important to note, however, that *Hawai'i One Summer, Veterans of War,* and *The Fifth Book of Peace* together comprise a distinct stage in the arc of Kingston's literary career, exploring themes that are not often associated with Chinese American or ethnic American writing, a fact that seems to trouble Kingston to lessening degrees as she grows older. For example, while pacifism has long been an important part of Kingston's personal life and a key theme in her earlier texts, she exhibits an increasing commitment to foregrounding her advocacy of antiviolence and global peace in these later works. Along with her usual explorations of what it means to be a part of a Chinese American community, Kingston is also deeply invested in examining how individuals can work together to create communities centered around peace. Her goal in these books is to find a blueprint for putting together communities and relationships that can build and maintain peace for now and the future; she seems to suggest that it is only in seeking out peace that the traumas of racial injustice and exclusion can be healed.

Hawai'i One Summer

Kingston composed the essays that make up *Hawai'i One Summer* during the summer of 1978. She was working to complete *China Men* at the same time, but, according to the preface that opens *Hawai'i One Summer,* was still feeling depressed about the fallout from the Vietnam War, even though it had ended several years earlier. Kingston turned to these essays as a respite from her work on *China Men* but also in order to grapple with the anxieties she was feeling about US geopolitics. Her despair about the effects of the Vietnam War as well as the images and themes that were engaging her in *China Men* unwittingly affected Kingston's approach to and composition of the essays in *Hawai'i One Summer.* As Kingston notes in her preface, she only became aware of the sadness she was feeling and the extent to which it had permeated her writing when a reader asked her after publication why the volume was filled with so many allusions to death and suicide. Kingston attributes the presence of these images to her disquiet about war and violence more generally; however, I would suggest that these images of haunting and passing also capture the legacy of colonialism and exploitation embedded in Hawaiian history and culture, a legacy in which Kingston feels ambivalently complicit.

Hawai'i is an important place for Kingston personally for a number of reasons. She and her family lived there for almost two decades, arriving in the mid-1960s and not leaving until well after her literary career had been established in the 1980s. It is the place where she wrote her most famous works, and it is the place she called home when she gained fame. As Kingston notes in her preface, "Hawai'i was a good place for writing about California and China."[2] Although she never states explicitly why this was the case, one can presume that the geographical and emotional distance of Hawai'i from those locations that had defined her family and her childhood enabled her to write more effectively about them. However, her connection to Hawai'i runs deeper than the span of her own life. Two of her great-grandfathers traveled to Hawai'i—or the Sandalwood Mountains, as the Chinese called the state—in the nineteenth century to work as farm laborers on the sugarcane plantations in order to send money back to China. Unlike these ancestors, however, when Kingston, her husband, and her son first arrived in Hawai'i, working was the last thing they wanted to do. As peace activists fleeing the bubble of Berkeley's increasingly desperate antiwar movement, they did not initially look for jobs when they arrived. At the time, Kingston recounts, she and Earll felt that it "was the duty of the pacifist in a war economy not to work. When you used plastic wrap or made a phone call or drank grape juice or washed your clothes or drove your car, you ran the assembly lines that delivered bombs to Vietnam" (15).

The move to Hawai'i was very much tied to their antiwar activism and their determination to live in as disconnected away from the US war machine as possible. But their arrival in Hawai'i did not mark the end of their disillusionment with the war and its opponents. Spending time with the enlisted men and seeing them in their daily lives forced Kingston to call into question the political motivations of the peace movement. She realized that the antiwar movement was as likely to exploit the soldiers (albeit in very different ways) as the government who was shipping them off to fight. When Kingston volunteers at a local church to support soldiers and sailors who have gone AWOL from base, she discovers that these men go AWOL not because they are opposed to violence or have some kind of philosophical opposition to the war but simply because they are dissatisfied with some mundane aspect of military life: they do not like their officers; they hate the food; or they want a break from the boredom of their daily regimen. In her attempts to make conversation with the soldiers, Kingston realizes that they are poorly educated, semiliterate, and from economically deprived backgrounds. In these conversations, she cannot shake the feeling that the "peace movement was using them no less than the government was" (18). Although they have no more desire for peace than they do for war, Kingston feels uncomfortable that the antiwar movement is holding them up as symbols of resistance to the war.

Problematically, even though Kingston believes that the men are being used, she nevertheless blames them for the situation they find themselves in. Kingston's attitudes toward these men reflect her own blind spots regarding class and educational status, prejudices that she displays in other works, in particular in *China Men*. Kingston's emphasis on the soldiers' ignorance, their lack of intellectual engagement with the world around them, and their desire for material comforts suggests that in her opinion they do not deserve to be associated with the peace movement. (She also doesn't seem to recognize that their refusal to serve because of a lack of palatable food or the hostility of repressive commanding officers might constitute acts of political resistance as principled as refusing to fight in an unjust war.) Kingston never considers the possibility that the soldiers' apathy toward the war might stem from a lack of opportunities they had—she does not see their apathy as the result of the institutional inequities that consign poor young men to the military but rather the result of their stupidity and laziness as individuals. She dismisses their ignorance as a result of their own failings rather than the product of graver social injustices within the nation.

Kingston's interactions with enlisted men is just one example of the vague discomfiture that creeps into her narrative of Hawai'i. The Kingston family come to Hawai'i expecting it to be a tropical escape from the troubles of the "real world," but what they discover is they have moved into the very heart of the US military industrial complex. Whereas in Berkeley it was rare to see soldiers in uniform or military equipment, in Honolulu, both are ubiquitous. Kingston's shock at the pervasive military presence in Hawai'i reflects what historian Simeon Man calls Hawai'i's "obscured centrality to the US war in Vietnam."[3] Man goes on to note that Hawai'i served a crucial purpose in national narratives of racial liberalism: its incorporation into the United States as the fiftieth state in the Union both "obscured the history of US imperialism in the islands [and] manifested . . . renewed forms of colonial state violence in Hawai'i and elsewhere in Asia."[4] Kingston's profound sense of unease with her experiences in Hawai'i—beginning with her interactions with US military personnel but also extending to her descriptions of racist place names on the Island and her relationship with native Hawaiian writers and activists—reflects her unarticulated sense of Hawai'i as a site for "the mutual formation of race and US Empire."[5]

Kingston never directly connects the turmoil of her life as a resident of Hawai'i with the violence wrought by the US state and its military, but the islands' history of colonization and occupation is never far from the surface of her text. Kingston notes that "the Navy uses Kaho'olawe for bombing practice, not recognizing it as living, sacred earth. We had all heard it, the voice our island singing" (33). In evoking Kaho'olawe, a well-established training ground for bombing runs by the US Navy, Kingston makes visible briefly Hawai'i's history as a land of economic and military exploitation, a staging ground for US imperial ambitions in the Pacific and Asia. If the Pacific has the been the "proving grounds" for the United States in terms of its global dominance and military ambitions, then Hawai'i has been the launching pad.

However, Kingston's identification with Hawai'i in opposition to the US state is a fraught and complex one. While Kingston speaks with respect and love of Hawai'i's history, geography, and cultural heritage, she is fully aware of her own "outsider" and "haole" status within the community. Kingston writes that on a visit to the Big Island, Pele says to her in a dismissive tone, "So you call yourself Woman Warrior, do you?" At the same time, she feels that the Hawaiians are silently admonishing her when she hears them say, "You have taken our land. Don't take our stories" (xii). Ironically, what this means is that while Hawai'i was a good place to write about China and California, it was not a good place for "writing about Hawai'i. I felt the kapu[6]—these are not your stories to write; these myths are not your myths; the Hawaiians are not your people. You are haole. You are katonk.[7] My great grandfathers, one on my mother's side, one on my father's side, and my paternal grandfather lived and worked in Hawai'i. Even so, they were not kama'āina, and I am not kama'āina" (xii).[8] These are surprisingly definitive statements from an author who has long advocated and reveled in ambiguities regarding her own identity. Despite historical and familial ties to Hawai'i, Kingston does not consider herself a local. Perhaps this is because even though she and her family have lived and worked in Hawai'i—sometimes for years—they have never considered it home, and while they endured privations on the islands—especially the great-grandfathers—these had more to do with their Chinese identities rather than anything to do with their locale. Kingston does not delve into the reasons why she does not identify this way, and the history of military and colonial invasion of the islands is only hinted at in the volume and never drawn out directly.

Kingston nevertheless feels a connection to Hawaii albeit one that is riven by guilt and confusion regarding her status. At a conference of Hawaiian writers, Kingston states that she is "humbled when Ozzie [Oswald] Bushnell, author of *Ka'a'awa,* said that if 'us local kids' don't write the Hawai'i novel then 'the outsider' will come in and do it. I guiltily identified with this 'outsider'" (47). Kingston's guilty association with the "outsider," even though she is being included with the locals, stems from a number of issues: that she only came to

Hawaii because she thought it represented an escape from America's wars of racial violence, because she is a Chinese American woman from the mainland, because she herself doesn't really have access to the histories or experiences of the Hawaiian peoples. There are no talk-stories about Hawai'i, no places in which to root herself.

This buried history of military intervention and imperial ambition manifests itself in the text via the images of death and suicide that pervade *Hawai'i One Summer.* Kingston attributes the presence of these tropes as the result of her own depression regarding the aftereffects of the Vietnam War, but it seems just as likely that her representation of death (in the forms of ghosts and hauntings as well as discussion of suicide and trauma) echo Hawai'i's history of exploitation and violence. Her own inability to connect comfortably with Hawaii is in stark contrast to her son. At one point, Joseph is plagued in his childhood by voices that only he can hear; he tells his mother that there are spots within the house that are "hot" or "cold." Kingston responds with the cultural remedies that she learned from her mother and that she depicted in *The Woman Warrior:*

> I pulled [Joseph's] ears while calling his name and address the way my mother did for us after nightmares. He helped me seal the closet door with good Chinese words on red paper. We found a cross that had been part of a theatrical costume, also an ankh and scarab, replicas from the Metropolitan Museum of Art, and hung them from the doorknob. We picked ti leaves and strewed his room with them (56).

Her attempts to ground her son via the Chinese American techniques her own mother used on her do not really work; it is only when a Thai friend of the family gives Joseph a small Buddha that he sleeps with on his pillow that the nightmares and voices stop. Although these incidents terrify Kingston, they also indicate to her that her son has a connection with forces (whether supernatural or cultural or something else, she does not specify) that are powerful but not understandable to her: "In a way it's a shame to have him put his powers away, fold his wings, but those abilities are not needed in America in the twentieth century" (57). Kingston does not specifically locate these "powers" within her family Chinese American history, and the story seems to suggest that her son is forging a connection with spaces and histories on Hawai'i that she cannot access in the same way. It is noteworthy that Hawai'i is a place where Joseph can feel these forces that his mother cannot feel or comprehend. In this anecdote, Kingston is once again the outsider, but her son, we learn later, is not. Joseph chooses to remain in Hawai'i after she and Earll return to California and continues to live there as an adult. In other words, Kingston's outsider status is not bequeathed to her son, who seems very comfortable with his life in Hawai'i.

Finally, *Hawai'i One Summer* offers the reader a glimpse into Kingston's attitudes toward the art and act of writing precisely at the time of its composition, she is in the midst of writing *China Men*. She is only two years removed from the phenomenal success of *The Woman Warrior*. For most of her professional life in Hawai'i, Kingston was a high school English teacher, encouraging students to write. So it is not surprising that her writing and the process of writing are very much the focus of this volume. She reflects on the writing teachers she has had in her life and the very rigid way that they taught good "writing," which entailed copying poetic phrases down word-for-word from the blackboard and practicing good penmanship. Whatever ability or creativity Kingston cultivated for herself as a writer, it certainly did not find any spark in this kind of classroom. There is no attempt to encourage critical or creative thinking or expression, and students are evaluated on how exactly they can copy the handwriting of the writing instructor.

This portrait of a woefully unimaginative and uninspiring teacher contrasts with Kingston's depictions of Hawaiian writers, who, with a few short words, are able to evoke feelings and experiences that are difficult to quantify. For example, Kingston struggles to understand her son Joseph's love of surfing, an activity that she finds frightening. Initially, Kingston attempts to understand the thrill of surfing by asking Joseph himself, who is unable to articulate why he loves being in the water, and then her students, who are all also avid surfers but tell her that there "are no words" to describe what surfing means. Her frustration over their unwillingness to put into words what they feel frustrates the storyteller in her: "You can describe it," she tells them angrily. "Everything can be described. Find the words for it, you lazy boy. Why don't you stay home and read?" (67). Kingston then turns to professional writers to understand what it is like to surf in the waves. Gary L. Crandall writes that it's an "iridescent ride through the entrails of God" (72) while Reno Abellira writes of it in intimate, almost sexual terms, as a "rendezvous" between the wave whose "crest" reflects her "deepest longings" and the surfer who strives "to spend every second, enclosed, encased, sometimes fatefully entombed, and hopefully gleefully, ejected—Whoosh!" (71–72). Kingston's inability to understand the allure of the waves is reflected in her characterization of the ocean as "mindless." Her desire to understanding surfing through language (rather than by learning it herself, which one might expect) also suggests Kingston's abiding belief in narrative as a means of processing and understanding experiences that range from the quotidian to the mystical.

The Fifth Book of Peace and *Veterans of War, Veterans of Peace*

E. San Juan Jr. writes that the "trauma of the Vietnam disaster lingers in the collective psyche of the American body politic, as Kingston diagnoses it in her hybrid testimony conflating fiction and history, creative fantasy and destructive reality, *The Fifth Book of Peace*."[9] While San Juan emphasizes the Vietnam War as the source-trauma for *The Fifth Book of Peace*, in reality multiple traumas form the core of the book's construction and themes. *The Fifth Book of Peace* emerged from a fire, specifically, the Oakland-Berkeley hills fire that burned down Kingston's house and decimated her neighborhood of Rockridge in October 1991. The house burned while she was in Stockton, attending funeral ceremonies for her father, who had died the previous month. In *China Men*, Kingston implies that Chinese America emerged from the ruins of the San Francisco fire of 1908. It was from those flames that Chinese men were able to forge—as in create and fake—a history for themselves in this country. She could not have known that her own life would be consumed by fire as well and that a new life would spring from those flames. The effects of that fire can be seen throughout *The Fifth Book of Peace*, both in terms of the themes and narratives that Kingston sets down and in terms of its structure. As Polly Shulman writes, this new book is a "strange, scarred thing, pieced together from fragments, smelling of smoke and anguish. Its power lies in its pain, but readers expecting the vivid characters and stories of her earlier work will be disappointed. Only the rewritten section, 'Water,' is fiction; the three other parts, 'Fire,' 'Paper' and 'Earth,' are memoirs that often have the incomplete, almost aimless feel of journal entries."[10] Shulman's review is characteristic of the critical response to the book, which tends to be marked by confusion and disappointment. Confusion because of the book's "incomplete feel," and disappointment because of the absence of the memorable characters and scenes that had appeared in Kingston's previous works. The layered storytelling of *The Woman Warrior* or *China Men*—filled with historical or imaginative details—gives way to the abstract philosophical ruminations of an aging Buddhist feminist. In this regard, *Fifth Book of Peace* marks a shift in Kingston's writing, turning toward questions of ethics, peace, and morality, as well as maintaining an interest in the areas of identity and community. John Whalen Bridge calls *The Fifth Book of Peace* "a form of engaged Buddhism."[11] However, the explicitly ethical and activist aim in this book also seems to throw some readers off. David Eubanks argues that the book's notion of "peace" is moralistic and therefore results in a much more conventional book, despite its seeming questioning of binaries and fragmented writing style.

Part of the reason why *The Fifth Book of Peace* seems to stump readers is because even more so than Kingston's previous titles, it defies any kind of generic expectations. There is no one narrator to unify the disparate sections, and rather than blending memoir with fiction to create a seamless narrative that raises questions about the difference between truth and fiction, as she does in *The Woman Warrior,* Kingston divorces her first person memories of the fire and its aftermath from the story of Wittman Ah Sing into distinct chapters. The book she imagined prior to the fire—the lost "Fourth Book of Peace"—is "plunked" (to borrow a term Kingston used to describe how she incorporated "The Laws" chapter in *China Men*) into the new version of the book with no exposition or transition. The first chapter of *The Fifth Book of Peace,* titled appropriately "Fire," recounts Kingston's frantic and ultimately futile attempts to get to her house and save her manuscript in progress—the "156 good pages" that made up the "Fourth Book of Peace." "Paper," the second chapter, is Kingston's description of the three mythical Chinese Books of Peace and her attempts to trace them through history. According to Kingston, there were "a long time ago in China," three Books of Peace, which were burned deliberately. Kingston asks a range of people if they have heard of these Books of Peace. She notes that she asks politely and cautiously, because she does not want to force scholars to "admit in front of colleagues that there's a classic they didn't know."[12] Some respond to Kingston's questions by telling her that no such books ever existed or that what she calls Books of Peace are really something else. Chinese scholars such as Wang Meng tell Kingston that since she "imagined Books of Peace . . . you are free to write whatever you like. You write them yourself" (52). "Water," the third chapter, represents Kingston's attempts to reconstruct the original manuscript; unlike the other chapters, it is fiction, and it continues the story of Wittman Ah Sing as he, his wife Taña, and their son move to Hawai'i to seek "sanctuary during the War in Viet Nam." Chapter four, "Earth," chronicles life after the fire with Kingston running her writing workshops for veterans across the country and sharing the poems and words of the many veterans who have become her friends and travel companions. A brief epilogue rounds out the volume.

A large portion of the book is devoted to the destruction of Kingston's manuscript. "Fire" is the first chapter, and fire is what defines this book and altered its structure. In her description of the afternoon that her house burned down, Kingston writes that as she was racing around her city streets, trying to find an access point to her neighborhood, all she could think was that she only needed one minute in the house; one minute to grab her book which was "in a wine box" in the living room and then rush upstairs to save the "gold and jade that my ancestresses had been able to keep safe through wars in China and world wars and journeys across oceans and continents" (5). Police roadblocks are the first set of obstacles; then, after slipping past barriers and police officers, she finds her once familiar neighborhood a maze of downed power lines, flaming trees, and burnt out homes. She gives up her quest to get to the house when she realizes that from her vantage point near the bottom of her street, a neighbor's flagpole is visible, meaning that her house, which should have obscured the view, no longer exists.

Kingston's interpretation of the proximity of the fire to her father's death is that her father "is trying to kill me, to take me with him. At this morning's funeral fires, we burned gifts and provisions for him, but it was not enough, and he's angry. He wants more—my book, all my books, my house, and neighborhood—and is taking more—my cities, Berkeley, where I teach, Oakland, where I live" (14). This image of a voracious and vengeful ghost, one who is not satisfied with the offerings made by those he left behind, is a familiar one to readers, recalling the No Name Aunt of *The Woman Warrior.* But Kingston's gloomy notion that the fire represents a dissatisfied-in-death father seeking revenge is countered by her mother who tells Kingston, "Your BaBa saved you!" According to Brave Orchid, Kingston's father "kept you busy and safe here [in Stockton]. If not for him, his funeral, keeping you home in Stockton, you—I know you—you would have been in a cloud of reading or a cloud of writing. . . . Your BaBa saved your life" (24). Kingston acknowledges that her mother's way is "the right way of seeing my father, not the father-god of the Americas who hunts his children and burns things with his anger, but BaBa, who used his funeral to save my life" (24). This is a characteristic moment in Kingston, offering two different interpretations for a single event, with Kingston acknowledging the "right way" of viewing events is her mother's. Note though that although Kingston recognizes this is the "right way," she does not come out and say that this is what she herself ultimately believes. Nevertheless, the moment seems different to me from Kingston's other narratives that are riven with disavowals of authorial power, since she gives the more loving or positive interpretation ("your BaBa saved you") the last word.

This kind of revision of previously told tales happens in other ways as well. In describing her father's journey from Cuba to New York City in *China Men,* Kingston emphasizes her father's fear, physical discomfort, and claustrophobia. The narrative makes clear that by agreeing to be transported to the United States in this way, the father is risking his own life. In *Fifth Book of Peace,* however, this same event is told in a strikingly different way. Rather than emerging from a crate on a ship in New York Harbor, traumatized by what he has endured, Kingston's father lands and discovers that Charles Lindbergh has completed his famous flight from New York to Paris. His ebullient response—"So—both of us did it!" (28)—differs radically from previous versions of this story. Here the tone is triumphant, equating Lindbergh's historic trip and BaBa's personal one. This equation, while presenting her father in a similarly heroic mode as the national hero Lindbergh, strikes a reader of *China Men* as dissonant, since the situations dictating the travel the two men undertook could not be more different. This version of BaBa's arrival into the United States is also much more conventional in that it presents the immigrant's journey as an adventure, one that represents him as a pioneer who dared to forge a new life for himself. This is the kind of US triumphalism that Kingston has tended to avoid in her earlier works.

Kingston's shift to another key in recounting these stories reflects the tremendous transformation her own life has undergone postfire. A few days after her initial attempt to reach her burning home, Kingston and two friends sneak back into the neighborhood (now more heavily and strictly guarded by the police) to try to see what has survived. The house is destroyed, but they are able to salvage some jewelry and personal mementos from the ashes. The situation is still dangerous: one friend burns the bottoms of his feet through his shoes after trudging through the thick ash in Kingston's house and the other winds up with a bloody nose from inhaling the residual soot and particles. Despite the destruction, Kingston is able to locate her book. The moment of discovery is described in religious terms, as one of transformation for the book and for Kingston herself. The scene also evocatively highlights how perilous the process of metamorphosing stories into text can be. She finds herself touching the "ashes of my Book of Peace" under an "unroofed sun" (34). These ashes, which recollect the ashes of a human body, have been blanched white by the fire, reminding Kingston of the words that she has written even though the pages no longer contain any words themselves. Kingston emphasizes the corporeality and materiality of the book's remains: the burnt pages are like "feathers" or "white eyelashes" with "vanes" that branch "into infinitely tinier vanes" (34). This description of the book's corporeality is in tension with its status as a "ghost"—the remnant of a living thing. Kingston describes how fire transforms paper that was once wood back into wood again, how it transforms ink into powder. Even the gentle touch of her finger against the ashes causes these remains to disintegrate even further, into "powder," into "airy nothing" (34). Kingston's placing of her hand on the manuscript resembles an act of benediction—a letting go or accepting of what has been lost.

The ritualized manner in which Kingston interacts with the ashes of her book suggests a funeral rite, the same kind that she had been participating in with her father's death. Her description of the book reads like an obituary:

"The Fourth Book of Peace, the book I was working on—156 good, rewritten pages that burned in the fire—was fiction. I was making up characters who use peace tactics. It had to be fiction, because Peace has to be supposed, imagined, divined, dreamed. . . . I hadn't gotten near the happy ending yet, which would be a happy ending to the Viet Nam War. The happy ending was to be reached with no violent action, no violent conflict, no apocalyptic climax" (61). And just as her father's death allows her to let go of some of her fears—first and foremost, the fear that her father will be deported—so too does the death of this version of the book wreak changes in Kingston's life. Kingston discovers that after the fire she cannot "re-enter fiction" in the same way (and indeed, *The Fifth Book of Peace* contains the last bit of fiction that she has ever published). Writing has become an intensely personal endeavor that she undertakes "for nobody to read but me," a possible explanation for why she makes the switch from prose to poetry (62). After the fire, she finds that she writes as she did when she was a young girl, out of necessity and comfort, and revels in her use of the "selfish first person" perspective. She feels free to "write diarylike, okay to be formless, no art, no good English" (62). While she no longer worries about how readers will respond to her writing, she also realizes after the fire that she no longer wants writing to be a solitary process. She wants her next Book of Peace to be constructed by a community of like minds.

The fire clearly had an enormous impact on Kingston personally—coming as it did on the heels of her father's death—and professionally, since it destroyed a work in progress. What is also clear although less obvious is the psychological effect of the fire on Kingston's writing philosophy. I would argue that the fire represents a profound shift in Kingston's writing—that the works that Kingston crafts after the fire are substantially different in theme and voice and direction than the works published prior to the fire. After the fire, Kingston moves away from fiction, becomes more interested in language as poetry, less concerned with the technical aspects of that form of communication. For Hsu Shounan, the Oakland-Berkeley fire is an event, defined by Alain Badiou as an "unpredictable and incalculable supplement to a situation."[13] As Hsu describes, such an event "compels [a person] to decide a *new* way of being."[14] A subject is constituted because of how he or she decides to be "faithful" to an event—"making inquiries about how to transform a situation according to the revelation of the event."[15] The fire triggers within Kingston a desire to make a shift in her writing that reflects the trauma and loss that she has already endured. But she also sees it as a return to a different self, one that is less concerned with the social consequences of writing and more interested in the communal possibilities that it offers.

The fire marks a definitive change in Kingston's writing life, but *The Fifth Book of Peace* still contains within it the remnant of what was lost. The chapter titled "Water" is Kingston's reconstruction of the burned book. In it, Wittman and his young family move to Hawai'i to escape the presence of the Vietnam War. Just as the Kingstons did, the Ah Sings—Wittman, his wife Taña, and their son Mario—realize that living in Hawai'i only brings the war that much closer to them; what was an abstract concept in Berkeley is now fully embodied in Honolulu. In departing California, Wittman feels exhilarated and guilty: exhilarated at the prospect of breaking with the life he has previously known and guilty about who he is leaving behind and why: "Always ambivalent, Wittman, escaping America, felt bad forsaking his people. America is over. He hadn't had the nerve to break the news to the *campesinos*" (68). Any sense that the family is leaving behind hostility and racial politics is dashed on the plane ride: they encounter a woman across the aisle who calls them "haoles and kachinks" and informs them that they are even worse than the tourists who visit Hawai'i in such droves. The anxieties that Kingston expressed in *Hawai'i One Summer* regarding her own outsider status and the possibility that she—as a mainland Chinese American—is somehow perpetuating the exploitation of Hawai'i is fully realized in *The Fifth Book of Peace*.

That Kingston is exploring her own anxieties regarding race and inclusion through the character of Wittman Ah Sing is particularly noteworthy. The Ah Sings journey from Berkeley to Hawai'i is clearly patterned after Kingston's, even down to Wittman and Tana's desire not to be employed once they reach the Oahu. (In the text, Wittman and Taña argue over who will work and who will be unemployed and thus have the leisure to practice his or her art—both want the freedom of unemployment first. Kingston does not reveal whether that argument was based on one she had with Earll.) Kingston chooses to fictionalize her own life experience through Wittman (as opposed to another character from her canon, or to write autobiographically), a character who one would think embodies many of the attitudes regarding identity and community that are oppositional to her own. Given Wittman's superficial similarity to Kingston's critical nemesis Frank Chin, why does Kingston identify herself repeatedly with Wittman?

Our surprise over Wittman's continuing presence and influence stems in my opinion from a critical misapprehension of Kingston's work. Readers—particularly within the academy—have simply overdrawn and overemphasized the parallel between Wittman and Chin. By reading Wittman only as a doppelgänger for Chin, we miss the extent to which Kingston uses Wittman to work out evolving ideas about the nature of identity and community that have very little to do with the personal nature of Chin's attacks against her. Although Kingston has acknowledged that Wittman "resembles" Chin, she also points out that she has never met Chin in person and that Wittman "resembles a lot of other people as well" *including herself.* This last point is an important one. Kingston notes that she and Chin are the same age, that she grew up in the same milieu as Chin, was politicized at the same university, worked with some of the same professors as Chin, and was active in a similar social and political scene. When she writes about herself, Kingston thinks that many readers assume that she is writing about Chin. In other words, Wittman is modeled after Chin only insofar as Chin's experiences represent the experiences of many Chinese Americans in the late 1960s in San Francisco.[16] It is ironic that with all of the attention paid to the Chinese American pen wars and whether or not Kingston's works can be categorized as nonfiction, no one has really stopped to theorize Wittman as an autobiographical figure for Kingston. But that is exactly what *The Fifth Book of Peace* compels the reader to do.

"Water" presents the burned book in the form it was in just before the fire; or, to be more precise, "Water" is Kingston's memory of the book as it was before the fire. She seems to have made no attempt to complete the novel as she originally conceived it. At the start of "Earth," which is the chapter that follows "Water" in the book, Kingston writes "There! That's what I wrote during two years of living at friends' houses after the fire. . . . I wrote past the place where the burned book left off. But found no happy ending" (241). If, as she suggests, the experience of the fire altered her attitude toward fiction irrevocably, then it would stand to reason that her desire to finish the book as a fictional work was altered as well. "Water" thus acts as a memorial to not only the lost book but also Kingston's former identity as a writer. Kingston's transformation as a writer is precipitated by an incredibly tragic event, which is why she doesn't celebrate it as a "happy ending," but it nevertheless altered her literary and personal path in ways that she could never have anticipated.

The chapter "Earth" is an account of Kingston's life after the fire, crashing with friends while her house is rebuilt, trying to write again, receiving stories from Vietnam War veterans answering her call to send her stories of peace, and running her workshops on "Reflective Writing" in a variety of locales across the country. During this period, Kingston's mother Brave Orchid becomes increasingly frail and is going blind. She moves into a small house trailer in another daughter's backyard and calls it a *soo hong,* or a "home where sojourners can stay for free" (349). She wants to allow villagers to stay there when they are traveling. They name the *soo hong* after Maxine's father but because calling the house *Soo Hong Hong* would be repetitive, they just call it *Soo Hong,* which Kingston translates as "Community Community" (349). After the fire, community building also consumes Kingston's professional life, as she travels around the world to share the stories of combat veterans and tries to conceive of different ways of building a peaceful community of mindful individuals. Near the end of the chapter, Kingston journeys to France with a group of veterans and her husband to participate in a retreat held by the famous Buddhist monk Thích Nhất Hạnh. A crew from the BBC follows the group for a program on writers crossing national borders. During her stay in France, Kingston chants another version of the Woman Warrior myth, which she notes she has previously told as a "women's liberation story and a war story" (391). The latest version she shares is one that emphasizes homecoming, for it is only now that she understands that the myth of Fa Mook Lan is fundamentally about a soldier returning home. It is fitting that the chapter then ends with the death of Kingston's mother. With her mother at peace, with her dream of a *soo hong* completed, and with Kingston's own house finally completed, Kingston writes that her mother's teachings have "stopped wars years hence." The notion that her work has ended wars that were to have happened in the future reflects Kingston's strong belief in the creative powers that communities can wield in the name of peace.

Although it is a separate and very different kind of text, *Veterans of War, Veterans of Peace* represents a coda to *The Fifth of Peace,* the culmination of the themes introduced in the last chapter of *The Fifth Book of Peace.* Given Kingston's stature in the literary world, it is perhaps surprising that she has not been more involved in these kinds of editorial endeavors; it is perhaps doubly surprising that her only edited volume consists of works by nonprofessional authors, and former soldiers at that. But Kingston's work with veterans is obviously one that she believes not just professionally but also personally and politically, and it has been a long-standing commitment. Even before the fire that ravaged her home, Kingston had been working for years with various veterans and Buddhist organizations to run the "workshop/community/sangha" in locations across the country. While more than five hundred veterans have participated in the workshop nationwide, a core group of about thirty have meet four times a year in Northern California to meditate, workshop, and talk. What Kingston describes is not a writer's group but rather a community; exactly the kind of community, in fact, that she hopes to create after her novel on the Fourth Book of Peace burns. The writing group is the model for the kind of artistic, political, and cultural community that she valorizes and writes about in *The Fifth Book of Peace.*

Kingston did not contribute any work to the volume, perhaps as a way of focusing the reader's attention on the experiences of the veterans themselves. In her brief introduction, she attempts to explain the impact of the Vietnam War on her life and writing. In previous interviews, she has talked about the war as evidence of the United States' racism against Asians. As well as being a geopolitical nightmare, it was a personal trauma: her own family was directly affected by the war, with two brothers and a brother-in-law drafted and another brother forced to flee to Canada. Kingston implies that America's prosecution of what she believed to be a racist war against an Asian country profoundly impacted how she viewed the United States and her place in it. In this, her reaction was not unusual. Lisa Lowe writes that the war in Vietnam defined the political awakening of a generation of Americans: "In a manner unprecedented in the twentieth century, the Vietnam War (1955–1975) shook the stability and coherence of the United States' national understanding of itself. An 'unpopular' war contested by social movements, the press, and the citizenry, a disabling war from which the United States could not emerge 'victorious'—there is perhaps no single event in this century that has had such power to disunify the American public, disrupting traditional unities of 'community,' 'nation,' and 'culture.'"[17] For Lowe, the war was a profoundly destabilizing event, one that made visible the fissures and conflicts that lurk underneath the surface of American exceptionalism. But it also had a destabilizing effect on Asian Americans who were already exposed to anti-Asian racism and exclusionary policies within the United States.

Kingston proposes to heal the breach between American combat veterans and the Vietnamese people through writing and Buddhist meditation. She positions herself as the one who can enable such a reconciliation to occur, allowing her to claim some agency over an event that clearly left her feeling vulnerable and alienated. In her work with veterans Kingston has propounded a philosophy of peace that sounds remarkably like her attitude toward literature and writing. No notion of peace is eternally valid, and like anything else, peace as a concept is historically contingent and defined by individuals and communities through a constructive process. In *The Fifth Book of Peace,* Kingston writes that the "images of peace are ephemeral. The language of peace is subtle. The reasons for peace, the definitions of peace, the very idea of peace have to be invented, and invented again" (402).

Veterans of War, Veterans of Peace is an attempt to invent and reinvent peace by the very men and women who were most involved in the prosecution of the war. Kingston's belief that "We tell stories and we listen to stories in order to live" motivates the volume.[18] By telling their war stories, these veteran-writers serve as warnings to those who were not combatants about the costs—physical, psychological, and emotional—of war. Kingston writes in her introduction, "Tell the truth. And so make peace" (3). Far from being messengers of war, these former soldiers have become messengers of peace. These sentences also reflect an intensifying ethos on Kingston's part regarding writing's spiritual as well as political work; as she has gotten older, these words have become a mantra for understanding her own literary output.

CHAPTER 6

To Be the Poet and *I Love a Broad Margin to My Life*

According to its jacket cover, *To Be the Poet* is Kingston's "manifesto" on the role that poetry will play in the rest of her life. While the publicity for *To Be the Poet* implies that poetry represents a totally new direction in Kingston's work, in truth, there has always been a poetic quality to her prose. However, it has only been in the last decade that Kingston has made the formal transition from memoirist and novelist to poet. These later poetic works have not garnered the same kind of critical or popular attention as her prose works, and so there have been fewer interviews and articles surrounding their publication, and therefore fewer opportunities for Kingston to explain her rationale for the change. In *To Be a Poet,* Kingston suggests that her decision to rethink her literary identity stems from the fire that incinerated her home and the manuscript that would eventually become *The Fifth Book of Peace.* In *To Be the Poet,* Kingston consistently refers to *The Fifth Book of Peace* as the "longbook" rather than by its actual title, a substitution that suggests a certain emotional distance from the manuscript and even carries with it a hint of resentment. Rather than a manifesto, which implies declarations and avowals, confidence, *To Be the Poet,* with its mixture of poetry and prose exposition, reads more like an exploration or a rumination, filled with self-doubt, questioning, and thoughts on poetry as a process. Both *To Be the Poet* and *I Love a Broad Margin to My Life,* Kingston's most recent work and the book of poetry that followed *To Be the Poet,* represent a profound shift in Kingston's philosophy about the relationship between literature and her own life. Kingston has always been an autobiographical author, but these texts recalibrate the relationship between the personal and the literary, between lived experience and representation. The wall or walls that separate fiction and nonfiction are broken down, as they are in previous works, but these volumes represent the most public and self-conscious dismantling of those divisions. In writing *To Be the Poet* and *I Love a Broad Margin to My Life,* Kingston explores even more openly than before the connections that bind experience to representation.

To Be the Poet

That Kingston must herald her transition from prose to poetry and that her publishers feel compelled to advertise it as a huge shift in her career reflects how famous she is as a prose writer as much as it also represents her desire to establish her poetic process and voice. Ironically, it also suggests an uncertainty about how one goes about taking up on the mantle of poetry—that Kingston declared so publicly her switch from prose stylist to poet carries with it a vague sense that Kingston is hoping that saying something is true will make it so. (The volume is based on the William E. Massey Sr. Lecture in the History of American Civilization that Kingston delivered at Harvard University in 2000.) The questions that permeate *To Be the Poet* are: How does one become the Poet? Is it a matter of simply declaring oneself to be one, as Kingston rather brashly does on the first page of the volume? Where does the inspiration for poetry come from? How is the process of writing poetry different from the process of writing prose? The reader cannot also help but ask where this desire to write poetry came from, after a long and prosperous career writing prose. Indeed, Kingston's *desire* for the life of the poet seems to predate her *ability* to write poetry; at no point in her earlier works does she talk about dabbling in the composition of poetry. Based on *To Be the Poet,* she never even expresses any interest in writing poems until the time came to finish the "longbook." So what does poetry now enable or form that prose no longer can?

One answer to that question is that for Kingston, poetry might be the most effective vehicle for introspection and reflection. In that case, *To Be the Poet* is a meditation not only on how a subject *becomes* "the Poet" but what it means *to be* "the Poet." Kingston's poetry is highly self-conscious and self-reflexive, constantly interrogating her own poetic impulses. Throughout the volume, Kingston wonders where poetry comes from, how it emerges from an individual, or what the proper objects of poetic inspiration are. Her questions to established poets are touching in their sincerity and naiveté: "Whenever I meet a poet, I ask: How will poetry come to me? What are the ways?"[1] Kingston asks Alice Fulton and Hank De Leo for their "secrets" regarding poetry (51). She worries that lyric poems can only be written by the young and that at fifty-nine years and five months she is too old to even consider the notion. *To Be the Poet* is not, in other words, the outpouring of spontaneous emotion of a young romantic but the chronicle of a process, one that is riddled with self-doubt. It is an artistic endeavor that needs to be cultivated and shaped and one that is entirely different from writing prose.

It is striking that a volume that concerns itself with poetry as process starts in prose. In fact, most of the first chapter and a good portion of the second chapter is written in Kingston's prose, with poems (most unrevised according to Kingston) popping up on the pages but not filling them the way we should expect in a volume of poetry. It is only in the third chapter that we get to see a steady stream of poems from Kingston (although again, there is a fair bit of prosodic exposition intermixed with the individual poems). Kingston's uncertainty regarding poetry—and her reliance on prose to define it—is reinforced by the fact that she professes at the volume's start to not knowing whether the few poems that she has written and published in the past actually qualify as poetry. Kingston has written "what has passed for poetry" (14) in the form of diary entries that were used in an anthology of Buddhist poems, but she asks the reader to decide: "are they poems?" (14). These "poems"—brief lines out of a diary, noting mundane things like appointments, lunches with friends, and travel schedules—are presented in stanza form but Kingston's questioning of their status as poems forces the reader to consider more carefully what defines poetry. Kingston wonders: can a line from a diary be a poem?

It seems like the answer to that question based on the rest of *To Be the Poet* would be no. Kingston approaches poetry as a practice as well as an art, a state of mind and being that must be entered into if one is to produce poetry that *is* poetry. One might argue that it is because she believes so strongly that poetry is process that Kingston chronicles her own evolving poetic identity in *To Be the Poet*. In other words, if one considers *To Be the Poet* an account of a poetic process rather than a product of that process, the incongruity of using prose to describe poetry dissipates somewhat. As with most things in her literary life, Kingston is obsessed with parsing out and making clear what she does know from what she does not know from what she can never know. It is as if Kingston still feels more secure engaging in this kind of self-reflexive and self-critical process via prose rather than via stanzas and verse.

As she does in other texts, Kingston integrates her previous works into *To Be the Poet*—the "longbook" that she is on the verge of finishing (as I mentioned at the start of this section, a reference to the long-gestating and fire-scarred *The Fifth Book of Peace*, published the year after *To Be the Poet* in 2003) particularly hangs over this text, as it seems to represent the final version of a previous literary life from which Kingston is eager to move on. *The Fifth Book of Peace* seems valedictory to an entire phase of Kingston's literary life—as if she is shutting the door to the past and wants to explain to her readers why she is making this move. Kingston begins *To Be the Poet* by proclaiming "I have almost finished my longbook" and that now is the moment for her to turn to poetry. Her life as a writer of prose has meant sacrificing time with her child and with her husband; she associates prose with being a "workhorse" and with labor while being a poet is to be a "skylark," to have a life filled with ease and happiness (1).

Kingston clearly understands what the life of a prose writer entails, but what does it mean to be a poet? On a practical level, where does a poet find inspiration, how are her days filled, and what does the process of writing a poem look like? Kingston attempts to answer these questions in the first chapter, at times with tongue firmly in cheek. What is striking about this volume is the ebullient and strongly self-deprecating sense of humor that Kingston exhibits throughout the work. She seems particularly attached to the assumption that writing poetry is less difficult and more joyful than writing prose. When Gary Snyder tells her that "for some reason . . . the people who read poetry are shy to criticize it. Prosewriters get criticism and scrutiny. But readers of poetry are shy to criticize poets," Kingston rejoices. "*So,* poets are even free of critics!" (9). Allen Ginsberg's advice to her that the "first thought [is the] best thought" elicits delight from Kingston who is thrilled that "every spontaneous thought [can] count as poetry! No draft after draft like a draft horse" (10). And when Kingston decides to take a day to go visit her brother and sister-in-law, she revels in the fact that "I was already acting like the Poet. The prose writer of the longbook never goes on spontaneous outings" (21). In chapter two, when she finally sits down to meditate and put herself in the proper frame of mind to receive poetry, she finds herself thinking about unfinished chores and checking the clock ("I have been at this for half an hour" [32]). She is excited when she realizes that she is "writing in lines!" (33) and is thrilled that she is developing an instinct for where to insert the line breaks. She narrates her composition and editing process, including the lines of poetry that she writes, going over the "directions for poetry" that Ted Sexauer—a Vietnam War veteran, participant in Kingston's writing workshop, and Kingston's de facto poetry tutor—provided, explaining which ones that she will cut, trying to figure out a way to "integrate" her ideas and words together.

Besides poking fun at herself and the notion that poets' lives are filled with overflowing emotions, impulsive trips, and are otherwise free of critical disputation, Kingston's gentle self-mockery obscures somewhat the resentment that she expresses toward the career she has had until this moment. For the sake of her novels and books, she sacrificed time with her son, husband, and presumably other family members; she felt at times unhappy, unloved, and unloving; and she endured the criticisms of reviewers and fellow writers regarding her works. In previous works, Kingston has written sympathetically and movingly about the unrecognized labor of Chinese men in the United States; here, for the first time, she expresses some fatigue about the labor that has taken twelve years of life and consumed over one thousand pages.

Chapter two, "I Call on the Muses of Poetry," takes the form of a series of diary entries. These dated entries narrate Kingston's attempts to write poetry following a series of seven steps put forth by Ted Sexauer. Kingston initially feels unsatisfied with calling her "jottings" poems: she writes that she has a "prosewriter's desire for more story. For more" (29). Kingston sets up a dichotomy between poetry and prose, with the former representing absence and the latter representing presence, or even excess. It is the absence that makes Kingston uncomfortable at the start of the book, and her desire to fill in the gaps that she feels poetry leaves in its wake demonstrates her belief that narrative and text can reconcile or at least render tolerable the gaps and tensions within an individual subject and a community. Telling stories reflects Kingston's belief that writing and text represent a form of resistance, liberation, and even a "moral principle" (as she writes in *The Fifth Book of Peace*). However, later in the volume, when she seems to be more comfortable exercising her poetic voice, Kingston sings a slightly different tune, writing "Word or picture cannot show / the Reality of Cow" (106). As a poet, Kingston expresses her skepticism that text can capture or reflect the intricacies of experience, even if text is the only vehicle we have to communicate experience, express our identities, or resist injustices. We have seen both of these strains of thought in Kingston's writings before: on the one hand, a commitment to text as a way of working through political and social exclusion and historical erasure, and on the other hand, a recognition that words can only do so much to right those past injustices. The binary that Kingston struggles with in *To Be the Poet* does not get resolved; rather, the question lingers as one with which the reader must also grapple.

By the end of chapter two, the prose has dropped away, and we have lines of poetry beginning to dominate. "Spring Harvest" is the final chapter in the book, and in it, Kingston either briefly introduces each poem with a few lines of prose or appends her reaction to the poem. For example, in a poem titled "Another Waking Up," Kingston concludes a poem in which she expresses a desire "to put a bullet / through my throat" with a single sentence: "Oh no, such happiness cannot be poetry. I refuse that one" (71). Along with rigorously editing what she feels is the appropriate object of poetic language Kingston continues to try to master technical or formal poetic practices. For example, Kingston writes in all seriousness "I have discovered what stanza breaks are for.

In the space, breathe. Before and after the poem, breathe. I can pause, raise my hand, and conduct your breathing" (80). Stanza breaks do not exist solely as scaffolding for the poem's structure or as a sign of a poem's thematic development; for Kingston, they are meant to remind the writer and the reader to be mindful of his or her thoughts, body, and actions. Here we get the sense that the writing of poetry is a meditative act, one that brings her closer to the ideals that she espouses in *Veterans of War, Veterans of Peace* and at the end of *The Fifth Book of Peace.*

The final poem in *To Be a Poet* offers yet another retelling of the story of "Fa Mook Lan," the daughter who takes her father's place in battle, perhaps the most iconic, best-known story in Kingston's *The Woman Warrior. Publisher's Weekly* called this poem the "most effective" in the volume, and I would agree that it is certainly the most powerful and memorable, perhaps because it is one that does not focus on the daily workings of Kingston's own life.[2] Instead, this poetic version of Fa Mook Lan's story represents a return to the literary, the representational, and it is perhaps no coincidence that this is Kingston's most lyrical and meaningful poem. The Fa Mook Lan of this poem is very different from the Fa Mu Lan of *The Woman Warrior.* In the poem, she sits at her loom weaving when the call to war comes; there is no martial training, no fantastical adoption by the gods, no mystical superpowers, as there are in the earlier version. Fa Mook Lan takes on the "wretched life of a soldier," is wounded and bleeds, and spends so many years away from her home—crisscrossing the country and yet never being able to settle anywhere in it—that she misses the deaths of both parents. There is no family ready to welcome her warmly upon her return: no husband, no son, no grateful village. This description of Fa Mook Lan as a creative artist and as a dutiful daughter who never got to spend time with her family is reminiscent of Kingston's sketch of the burdens of her own professional and artistic life. In the poem, Fa Mook Lan is not lionized for her martial abilities but is followed home by her soldiers; while they wait for her, she steps inside her house to "dress herself in pretty silks, / and redden her cheeks and lips" (110). She finally appears before her army as a beautiful woman, telling them "I was the general who led you," to the general astonishment of her soldiers. She tells them that she is a woman, the war is over, and that they should return home. The poem ends with the somewhat ambiguous lines, "Beholding—and becoming—Yin—the Feminine, / come home from war. / Jik jik jik. Jik jik jik."

It is hard not to read the end of "Fa Mook Lan" as an allegory for Kingston's own transformation from prose stylist to poet, from Asian American warrior woman to elderly Vietnam War vets' writing coach. The readers who have followed Kingston from California to China and back again cannot believe that this writer who has been a leader and model no longer wants to play the part that we've come to expect. In interviews following the publication of *The Woman Warrior,* Kingston always expressed a regret that the warrior story of Fa Mu Lan was what she was most associated with and was what made her famous. This version of the Fa Mook Lan story seems to make amends for that previous association. At the end of *To Be the Poet,* Kingston tells us, her loyal readers, I guided you to knowledge and victory, now I must reveal who I really am and lead the life I want—so go home. Kingston suggests that she is no longer interested in presenting a certain version of herself to her readers; she has challenged us, given us insight with her prose, and now she wants to be herself, her true self—a poet.

I Love a Broad Margin to My Life

There are many ways of thinking about *I Love a Broad Margin to My Life:* as the elegiac meditation of an artist facing her mortality, as a poetic reunion of author with her most famous literary creations, as a reimagining in verse of the themes surrounding identity, violence, the power of narrative that have dominated Kingston's career. Unlike previous works, *I Love a Broad Margin to My Life* offers glimpses of Kingston's everyday life as a writer, as a war activist, as a daughter, a wife, and a mother. There is also a return to the familiar as Kingston revisits a number of themes and events that appear in earlier works. There are references to the No Name Aunt in *The Woman Warrior,* the Land of Women from *China Men,* and an extensive section in which Kingston imagines herself traveling to China with Wittman Ah Sing from *Tripmaster Monkey: His Fake Book* and *The Fifth Book of Peace.* However, these references are not a compilation of Kingston's greatest hits, nor are they an exercise in nostalgia or self-congratulation. Instead, Kingston rewrites, revises, and reconceptualizes these familiar figures to better reflect the personal and political investments of her later life. The reader is not comforted by the reappearance of these familiar characters but rather productively discomfited by how much Kingston has changed them. *I Love a Broad Margin to My Life* is elegy that doesn't fall into the trap of nostalgia.

Kingston's foray into poetry has occurred later in her career but her poetic endeavors have not been met with the same kind of acclaim or sales as her prose projects. Part of this is due to the fact that the public's interest in poetry is absolutely dwarfed by its appetite for prose. Even a writer of Kingston's reputation might find it difficult to find an audience for her poetry. Then there is the fact that Kingston's poetry has not been well reviewed; indeed, in the case of her poetry, the notices have been brief and less than enthusiastic. David Orr, writing in the *New York Times,* argues that while the *I Love a Broad Margin to My Life* has some "lovely" and "dry" moments, it is overall not a success. According to Orr, "the problem is twofold. First, Kingston appears to regard poetry less as a practice to be mastered than as a state of mind to be inhabited ('being the Poet'). Second, the book lacks a formal structure that can accommodate the burden of so many pages. The first factor leads the author to indulge in gooey mysticism that almost certainly would get cut—or toughened up—if she were working in her usual distinguished prose."[3] Orr thinks that the absence of structuring units within the book (whether based on stanzas, meters, or formal shifts) makes the poem seem to be nothing more than sentences broken up into short lines at random. While Orr is unimpressed with Kingston's poetic voice, he nevertheless has no problem calling Kingston a "Poet" in the Emersonian sense, meaning that he believes that she is actually much more of a poet when she is writing prose than when she is actually writing poetry. Reviewer Susana Rustin concurs with Orr, stating that she was "disappointed" by the new book, which had a "self-aggrandizing" air to it.[4] What both critics seem to suggest is that Kingston is more interested in or enamored with the image of herself as a poet than in the hard work of writing poetry that connects to her readership. Orr and Rustin point out that the absence of certain structures—both metrical and thematic—dulls the impact of her work and that her technical deficiencies and her seeming lack of awareness of poetic construction reduces Kingston's poetry to self-indulgent ramblings parading around as philosophical truths.

Leaving aside the personal vitriol that *The Woman Warrior* generated, these reviews of *I Love a Broad Margin to My Life* are undoubtedly some of the most tepid and dismissive of Kingston's career. I want to suggest that that they fail to take into account the ways in which this volume self-consciously calls attention to its poetic voice, how Kingston makes visible her attempt to take on the mantle of poet, a process that makes clear how important this new subject experience is for her but also reveals how uncomfortable she is with it. In a more sympathetic review that appeared in *Hyphen Magazine,* Manan Desai focuses on the book's thematics rather than Kingston's poetic technique, writing that *I Love a Broad Margin to My Life* "attempts to deconstruct the memoir by playing on the central tension between preservation and erasure."[5] While I agree with Desai that there is a tension within the volume between presence and absence, I suggest that the central trope of *I Love a Broad Margin to My Life* is what it means to form and re-form an identity (whether it is racial or artistic) when one is approaching the end of one's life, a time when many of us assume that a sense of self will have solidified.

Kingston's realization of her own mortality opens the volume. While Kingston makes mention of her more recent personal activities in some previous works and in interviews, *I Love a Broad Margin to My Life* provides perhaps the most personal and intimate account of Kingston's life in the present. She talks about her son Joseph, a musician and fellow artist, to whom she seems to be close; she thinks about aging and the effect it has on her looks; she travels to China with her husband Earll to revisit her parents' villages; and she feels guilty when she thinks about the sadness her mother must have felt when she—her eldest daughter—moved with her young family to Hawai'i in the 1960s effectively cutting herself off from regular visits with her aging parents. In this regard, *I Love a Broad Margin to My Life* seems like a more "traditional" memoir than either *The Woman Warrior* or *China Men,* offering a more transparent view of Kingston's life and thoughts in a narrative voice that seems more self-assured and less interested in querying its own authority or knowledge. The volume opens with Kingston thoughts about aging: "I am turning 65 years of age. / In 2 weeks I will be 65 years old. / I can accumulate time *and* lose time?"[6] The repetition of Kingston's impending birthday in the first two lines might be an example of some of the technical clunkiness that Orr and others have noted, but that repetition of an ordinary fact might also reflect Kingston's desire to resituate herself as an artist who is now a senior citizen. She notes that in aging, one accumulates time with the passage of the years, but also loses time as one approaches death. In a characteristic manner, Kingston reveals how the juxtaposition of loss with gain can only be reconciled via narrative.

Although she passed away years before this book was published, Brave Orchid continues to play an outsized role in *I Love a Broad Margin.* Indeed, there is a poignancy to Kingston's depiction of her relationship to her mother that is not as prevalent in *The Woman Warrior.* In *The Woman Warrior,* the narrator explains to Brave Orchid that when she is away from Stockton, which is filled with memories of her childhood, she doesn't "get sick. I don't go to the hospital. . . . I can breathe" (108). The narrator lists the litany of physical ailments that mysteriously emerge when she is back in her parents' home: the headaches, the medicines, the paranoia, and the insomnia all brought about, as the narrator explains, because she is constantly listening for the sounds of ghosts. The narrator of *The Woman Warrior* tells her mother that "I've found some places in this country that are ghost-free" (108). Even telling this to her mother gives the narrator a "spider headache," one that "spreads out in fine branches" over her head. She describes the guilt her mother lays upon her for not living at home as feeling like her mother has "open[ed] my head and my fists and crams into them responsibility for time, responsibility for intervening oceans" (108). The narrator notes that the unwillingness of Brave Orchid's children to live near the family home is payback for the fact that neither Brave Orchid nor her husband listened to their parents' own pleas to return to them in China. "Now they know how she felt," the narrator notes somewhat smugly (108).

But in *I Love a Broad Margin,* the years-long separation from her mother feels much more like a loss for both mother and daughter. Kingston mourns that she left her MaMa to attend college and then to live in Hawai'i, unable to visit very often because of the cost or distance. Upon every departure, Brave Orchid plaintively asks her daughter a question that Kingston initially translates as "How can I bear / your leaving?" before correcting herself and explaining that her mother actually asks "Can I seh doc your leaving?" (28). According to Kingston "seh doc" means "the pain of losing something valuable. / How can she *afford* my leaving?" (28). Kingston's second-guessing of her translation of her mother's words to her ("seh doc") is characteristic and familiar from Kingston's previous texts. The distinction between asking whether one can "bear" a loss versus "afford" a loss is a difficult one. Bearing a loss suggests enduring a loss but accepting it. Affording a loss suggests that the sufferer does not have another drop of grief to spare—that the limit has been met. Kingston goes on to note that "*Seh doc* sounds like *can write,*" which also sounds like her father's name, the father who also left Brave Orchid in China for fifteen years (28). What connects Kingston to her family is thus both loss and narrative. Kingston connects the loss of a beloved one with the ability to write as well as her father's own name, a series of links that suggests that the relationships between family, narrative, and loss are constitutive and imbricated. To feel a loss is to narrate that loss; to write of a father is to write of the loss he felt at leaving his family.

The regret that Kingston feels about abandoning her mother is palpable throughout this section of the poem. Every time she departs her parents' home as an adult, her mother blesses her with luck, and although her eyes are "large and all-holding" she sheds no tears at these departures (29). Kingston's guilt over causing her mother this kind of sadness might be something of a surprise to those who are familiar with her earlier works. Her representation of parental and maternal love in *I Love a Broad Margin to My Life* has mellowed, and her mother's expressions of love and care are more conventional: rather than cutting her daughter's tongue to make her a better speaker, she "look[s] after each child" with eyes that are "large and all-holding" and filled with unshed tears. Instead of calling her daughter a dog or piglet, instead of labeling her a ghost, she gives her a blessing.

There is a similar moment a few lines down, when Kingston imagines what it may have been like for her mother to leave China in 1939. Rather than focusing on what her mother went through, which is what Kingston does in *The Woman Warrior* and *China Men,* in this version of the narrative Kingston thinks about her mother's departure from China in terms of whom she left behind. She imagines her grandfather Ah Goong accompanying her mother to the village's border, and the tears he shed as he watches her walk away. The subtle shift in Kingston's description of these scenes of children leaving their parents suggests that she now sees these departures from the perspective of the one who is being left behind rather than from the perspective of the person leaving. It is partly a function of aging, but it is also a function of realizing what it means to lose a loved one when one is too old to follow that family member. Her own position within these family and migration narratives has shifted subtly, and her retellings of these stories reflect that change.

Although Kingston's relationship with her father is not portrayed to the same extent in *I Love a Broad Margin to My Life,* he too is depicted as having changed and softened with age. Kingston writes that her "Father had / a happy life," a characterization that seems surprising given the anger and frustration that he is often portrayed as feeling in *China Men* (19). Or perhaps it is Kingston who has changed with age? One gets the strong sense that Kingston herself approaches her parents and their foibles with more patience and compassion, and that the things that mystified her as a child and adolescent about her parents seem less important. Kingston also expresses regret that she never traveled back to China with her father. The reason that she never invited him to return is of course fear, fear that his "fake" papers would make it impossible for him to return to the United States if he left. Despite the fact that her BaBa has "lived in the Americas for over 60 years," he has never felt at "home" in the United States (190).

Kingston emphasizes that Baba "was a prisoner of barbarians," a reference perhaps to Ts'ai Yen, who appears at the end of *The Woman Warrior* and who is described in exactly those terms in that book. Ts'ai Yen's exile lasted over a decade, but BaBa's spanned for over sixty years. In this poem, Kingston positions BaBa—whose name implies loss and narrative, and who himself was a poet—as the wellspring of her creative endeavors. Even after decades and decades of living in the United States, after a life devoted to work and family, the family still feared that their BaBa could have been deported for his illegal entry into the country. It was this fear that initially kept Kingston from going back to China (even though her status as a citizen should have protected her), and it was this fear that prevented her from inviting her father to travel back to China with her. "We should've chanced going," Kingston writes regretfully, but the reality of US immigration laws and the anti-Chinese bias that lingers even over fifty years after Exclusion was lifted are too strong to overcome.

Kingston also revisits signal events that have already been represented in her previous, most famous publications. The Vietnam War is still very much on Kingston's mind, especially given the fact that she is now active in protesting the US involvement in Iraq (9). She revisits the "Big Fire" that burned her

Rockridge home nearly a decade earlier, the fire that destroyed her manuscript for *The Fourth Book of Peace*. Perhaps of most interest to her readers is the fact that Kingston revisits scenes from *The Woman Warrior,* traveling to her father's village. It is while eating with her distant relatives that she realizes that the well outside of the ancestral home is the one in which her No Name Aunt must have killed herself and her baby. Kingston is astonished that the well itself does not seem very deep and that the water seems to reach close to the top of the well. She states bluntly a grown woman "couldn't have possibly jumped into / a well this shallow and drowned" (169).

In interviews, Kingston has talked about visiting her father's village and seeing the home where the No-Name Aunt lived. In an interview with Paul Skenazy that I cited earlier, Kingston expresses relief and pride when she visits her father's village for the first time and discovers that all of the details that she included in *The Woman Warrior* regarding her aunt were accurate. She tells Skenazy, "I saw the well where [my aunt] drowned. And I felt really good because I found that the China I had imagined is very much like the China that's there."[7] Nowhere in that interview does Kingston talk about the well being too shallow for anyone to drown in. But here, in *I Love a Broad Margin,* Kingston offers the most extensive description of the scene of her unknown aunt and cousin's deaths, and the contrast between the well in the first visit and in this visit could not be more stark. Notably, Kingston does not reference that first visit at all; it is as if this visit is the first time she has ever laid eyes on the well that she made so famous. There are two sets of discrepancies here. The first, which Kingston herself points out, is between the well that Kingston imagined in *The Woman Warrior* and the well that exists in the village with water that is "ankle deep." The second, which Kingston seems to elide, is between the well of her initial visit to China and the well that appears in *I Love a Broad Margin.* These contradictory accounts of the well may simply be the result of dramatic license or a failing memory; or they could simply reflect Kingston's belief that such contradictions are part of the fabric of experience and narration. She is not returning to China and her family's village to authenticate the truth of her experiences as she once did decades ago; instead, she simply notes the inconsistency before moving on.

This is what is most striking about *I Love a Broad Margin to My Life:* its absence of any kind of wistfulness or yearning for the past, even though she is engaging in activities and travel that are bound to raise the ghosts of past stories and lives. The affective register that her title invokes is not matched in the expected ways by the text itself. Kingston does not portray her journey to her Chinese village or meeting with her family with any kind of sentimentality. There is no sense of a momentous homecoming or of a spiritual connection to her relations; this isn't *The Joy Luck Club.* Rather, she notes those that claim to be her family, whether because they long to be linked to a celebrity or simply because, as an American, she must be worth knowing. One of the women who claims kinship is a "crone / wee, shriveled to my size" who grabs Kingston's hand and makes the somewhat strange assertion that "You and I / are very related" (168–69). Although she only appears in a few lines, one gets the sense that this "wee crone" could be a double for an aging Kingston herself; they are related by blood but also perhaps in the same way as Kingston and the silent Chinese girl who so memorably appears in the final chapter of *The Woman Warrior.*

Kingston also meets half cousins who are partly of African descent, relatives that she mentions briefly in *The Woman Warrior* and *China Men*. One cousin in particular confuses Kingston, who wonders if she should call this woman "Elder Sister" or "Younger Sister" (178). In the next sentence, Kingston seems to suggest that making such a distinction is irrelevant given how tenuous the familial connection is between this woman and herself: she notes that this woman's father-in-law was not "really my mother's brother" because he was a son of a concubine as opposed to Brave Orchid who was the child of the "first wife" (178). Kingston's understanding of family is peculiar here since her mother and half-uncle *were* related by blood; she seems to give credence to the highly patriarchal notion that only the children of first or official wives "matter" in terms of family.

This grandfather, Kingston explains, had several wives, the third of which was from Central America, "whose skin was black, whose / jabber no one understood" (178). Kingston's use of the word "jabber" to describe how this ostensibly African-descended woman talked is problematic, suggesting of course that this ancestor spoke a gibberish that was not bound by the same kinds of grammars that rule official languages. This troubling racializing of the "dark-skinned" branch of her family also emerges in her description of her "boy cous-in-how-/many-times/removed" who looks as if he belongs in the tropics (178). Although the encounter is brief, there is also an othering of this line of the family on Kingston's part ("Besides her father-in-law was not / really my mother's brother"), a suggestion throughout the decades that their great-grandmother didn't belong in China the way that Kingston's line did. Again, at this stage in her life, Kingston is not interested in trying to forget connections of this kind with family that she does not know.

One character that she does know is Wittman Ah Sing, who again, makes an extended appearance in *I Love a Broad Margin to My Life*. It should be clear by now to a reader of Kingston that Wittman is the character to whom Kingston returns again and again in her narrative imaginings, as if she is not finished telling his story. Why Wittman is such an appealing literary companion for Kingston, discussed in a previous chapter, and why our surprise regarding his enduring presence in the Kingston canon says more about how we overemphasize certain kinds of narratives within Asian American studies (the Chinese American pen wars) at the expense of others. Wittman Ah Sing—more than the warrior woman or any China Man—is Kingston's proxy and counterpart. Throughout the middle section of *I Love a Broad Margin,* Kingston invokes Wittman as her traveling partner to China: "Wittman is going to China for the first time" (50). This line reflect the complexities of Kingston's relationship to her most obstreperous literary creation. Kingston seems proud in a highly competitive manner of the fact that she has traveled to China so many times in contrast to Wittman who has never seen China. But the fact that she compares herself to Wittman at all is also noteworthy. When she measures her own experiences with her Chinese American identity, she immediately thinks of Wittman.

There is also the fact that Wittman is a senior citizen, having aged just as Kingston has. Kingston writes that Wittman decides to abandon Taña and their marriage on his sixtieth birthday in order to undertake his trip to China. Before he goes, his family comes to bid him farewell; now it is Wittman's son Mario who is the young man, and Wittman who is the old one. In his conversation with Mario he explains why he wants to visit China: "I am curious to know / who I am alone among a billion three / hundred million strangers who look like me" (40). Despite his age and his mellowing, Wittman still calls himself "the Monkey of Changes" (40). His understanding of himself as Chinese has evolved since *Tripmaster Monkey;* he wants to see himself in relation to a global Chinese population rather than insisting so militantly on a Chinese American identity. The Wittman of *Tripmaster* would proclaim that he has no connection to the China of his ancestors, being four generations removed from the land of his ancestors, but the elderly Wittman wants to explore all aspects of his Chinese heritage.

But he has not changed completely. Despite the fact that his construction of Chinese American identity is more transnational in its scope, he still insists that America is "our nation." He regrets that he missed important historical events in China because he was "kept busy claiming" the United States from those who called him a chink or told him to "go back to China" (41). According to Wittman, the Chinese have earned their place both legally and symbolically within the United States because they made America the wonderful place it is today. Wittman asks rhetorically and defiantly, "Why should *we* leave?" (41). This rhetoric of Chinese American belonging is one that Kingston has consistently deployed since her first work. And Wittman takes great pains to explain that even though "my work establishing Asia America / is done," his departure "is not exile" (41). America remains his home, even if some of its inhabitants would rather see him go away. The trip to China allows Wittman to "act out my deep / down monkey nature" (41). Invoking the trickster figure of the Monkey King suggests that part of the motivation for this trip to China stems from the fact that it is unexpected of Wittman.

In going to China for the first time, Wittman again invokes the poetry of his namesake, Walt Whitman:

> Facing west from California's shores,
> Inquiring, tireless, seeking what is yet unfound,
> I, a child, very old, over waves, toward the house of maternity, the
> land of
> migrations, look afar,
> Look off the shores of my Western sea, the circle almost circled . . .

Walt Whitman was a referent for Wittman and an important trope within *Tripmaster Monkey,* but the citation of this poem "Facing West from California's Shores" is striking. Written on the eve of the arrival to the United States of a Japanese envoy, "Facing West" looks toward Asia as a kind of future in terms that are conventionally Orientalist at best, highly expansionist at worst. Whitman's rhetoric of American exceptionalism has always been an alibi for its acquisitive designs on its western and southern frontiers and then across the Pacific. Whitman's poet gazes at the East with an imperialist purpose—to seek what is "unfound" to the west of the United States—the Pacific and Asia.

> Long have wander'd since—round the earth have wander'd,
> Now I face home again—very pleas'd and joyous.
> (But where is what I started for so long ago?
> And why is it yet unfound?)

Kingston does draw a contrast between herself and Walt Whitman when she notes that she, unlike Walt Whitman, could never "wander" because she always had "responsible work to do, the teaching, the writing." As he is in *Tripmaster,* Walt Whitman is invoked as a contrast to Kingston and Wittman's experiences as poets and as travelers. But Kingston does not critique the imperialist agenda that is implicit in the poem. Just like Whitman in the poem, Kingston does not interrogate her own positionality in relation to China: a famous Chinese American author returning to her ancestral village with cameras and others in tow to visit her poorer and anonymous distant family members. To the Chinese villagers who greet her, Kingston's privilege is such that in their eyes, she probably has more in common with Walt Whitman than she does with any of them.

It is through Wittman that Kingston can explore most fully the relationship between narrative, identity, and community. Rather than freeing her from familial, communal, and cultural obligations, Wittman only roots Kingston more deeply into those kinship networks. Her identity is very much communal, wrapped up in family and neighborhood; these ties, while they have been richly explored throughout her work, seem at times to constrain her. Kingston writes that she needs a companion like Wittman, who, like the Monkey of Chinese legend is "unafraid and unembarrassed" to speak his mind to strangers precisely because he is a fiction, he is "free," meaning "he has no relatives" to whom he feels beholden or obligated (104). Fiction offers Kingston the freedom to be the kind of subject that she feels that she cannot be in her own life. Wittman is an alter ego, one who can speak his mind without embarrassing anyone (much less himself) and who can form attachments without regard to what others may think of him. Kingston, on the other hand, is very much a creature and creation of her community, and these ties cannot be cut no matter how far one stretches them. I noted earlier that Kingston's responsibilities to her "work," her "teaching," and her "writing" prevented her from ever becoming a wanderer (50). But one also gets the sense that she never "wandered" because it is impossible to wander when one feels a sense of responsibility to one's family and community.

Even though Wittman is not saddled with the same intense ties to the his community, Kingston nevertheless describes him almost as if he were a family member, writing that although she is leaving him in China, she does not want to kill him, or imagine him "sick and poor, destitute of health and money," without a way to get home or an identity to which to return (104). Instead, she wants to imagine him (and presumably, wants her reader to imagine him) in a "commune of our bohemian / dreams" (105). Finally, she is leaving Wittman behind, but she does not want to let go of the ideals that he and his generation represented. It is that shared sense of idealism that draws the two of them together, and even though Kingston may be leaving that behind her, she wants to leave part of it for Wittman. The passage reveals the sense of responsibility that Kingston feels toward her creation. What is more, she doesn't want to leave him without a ticket, passport, or identity, those signs of a citizen who belongs somewhere. Kingston wants to make sure he can find his way home, even if she can no longer keep him company on his travels.

It is ironic that Kingston is loath to "leave [Wittman] dying" given the fact that she does not have any compunction about sharing the news that her most famous creation—Fa Mu Lan, or Fa Mook Lan as she calls her here—died by her own hand. As the story of Fa Mu Lan opened Kingston's writing life, the story of Fa Mook Lan closes it. *I Love a Broad Margin* is actually Kingston's third telling of the myth. The first version of the story, recounted in *The Woman Warrior,* is about a warrior woman who is honored for her martial prowess and filial piety. The second version of the story from *The Fifth Book of Peace* is about what it means to come home from war. And the third version, the final version, narrated in *I Love a Broad Margin,* is the story of Fa Mook Lan's death. As Kingston writes, "I have broken the news that Fa Mook Lan / killed herself" (217). According to a paper that Kingston reads while at a conference at Notre Dame, "Fa Mook Lan killed / herself by hanging; she refused the emperor's / order that she become one of his wives" (217–18). The suicide of this figure, the heroine of a million feminist fantasies, is a shock. Kingston writes that "everyone who hears denies / that it happened. No. How? Why?" (217). That she has to kill herself for refusing to marry the emperor reflects the fact that even the most empowered woman in Chinese society must bow to patriarchal prerogatives or pay with her life. This has always been an underanalyzed aspect of the Fa Mu Lan story as it appears in *The Woman Warrior:* Fa Mu Lan is the idealized embodiment of patriarchal obedience even as she seems to break down certain kinds of gendered hierarchies. She bows to her in-laws upon her return from war and promises them that she will now serve and bear sons for them. That she willingly and happily capitulates to the social conventions she seemed to be breaking serves ultimately to strengthen those very norms.

Nevertheless, the fact that Kingston's readers initially respond with disbelief to the death of this fictional and mythic character speaks to how potent and powerful a figure Fa Mook Lan has been. When readers or colleagues ask Kingston "Why?," they are no doubt wondering why she felt the need to kill the character with whom she is most closely associated and who made her famous, a symbol of resistance and resilience, especially since there does not seem to have been any pressing personal or political reason for Kingston to do so. As usual, Kingston doesn't really provide any answers. After acknowledging that the source for this story is the People's Republic of China and that they may be writing a "revisionist history," she simply asks "Why continue to live?" (218).

Indeed, the story of Fa Mook Lan's suicide follows a list of friends and colleagues who have died in the four years it took Kingston to write *I Love a Broad Margin,* some famous (John Gregory Dunne, Quintana Roo, Jade Snow Wong, John Leonard, Grace Paley, Ron Takaki, Lucille Clifton, Howard Zinn), most not. That she includes within the pages of *I Love a Broad Margin* her own version of a book of the dead reinforces a sense that Kingston feels that she is near the end of her life and at the end of her own words. She wants to live long enough to finish a translation of her father's poetry, but she already knows that her love of and fascination with language is fading. It is a love and fascination that have seen her through the writing and publication of nine books, countless essays and interviews, documentaries, and writing workshops. With the close of this book, Kingston implies that she has earned a right to rest and observe the worlds that she has chronicled so engagingly for over forty years. Just as the Chinese attained their place in the United States by creating its myths and landscape, Kingston justifies and accepts her future silence by pointing to the stories that she has written. She will finally "become reader of the world" that she has written about for so long (221).

NOTES

Chapter 1: Understanding Maxine Hong Kingston

1. Kingston, "Opening Speech," 24.

2. Ibid.

3. Kingston is vague in her texts and interviews about these two children and does not reveal any further information about them.

4. Mandelbaum, "Rising from the Ashes," 51.

5. Ibid.

6. Horton, "Interview with Maxine Hong Kingston," 7.

7. Kingston, *China Men*, 126. All further references to this work will be cited in the text.

8. Roorbach, "Maxine Hong Kingston," 167.

9. Kingston, *Through the Black Curtain*, 6.

10. Martin, "Maxine Hong Kingston Takes Pride in Mixed Heritage," *Tell Me More*, NPR.org.

11. Robertson, "'Ghosts' of Girlhood," 26.

12. Islas and Yalom, "Interview with Maxine Hong Kingston," 21.

13. Moyers, "Maxine Hong Kingston," *Bill Moyers Journal*, PBS.org.

14. Robertson, "'Ghosts' of Girlhood Lift Obscure Book to Peak Acclaim," 26.

15. Huntley, *Maxine Hong Kingston: A Critical Companion*, 9; Kubota, "Maxine Hong Kingston," 3; Horton, "Interview with Maxine Hong Kingston," 9.

16. Leonard, "In Defiance of Two Worlds," C21. These words are still emblazoned on current editions of the book.

17. Loke, "The Tao Is Up," SM28.

18. Guthrie, "Maxine Hong Kingston Embarks."

19. Huntley, *Maxine Hong Kingston*, 65.

20. There are several worthy book-length histories that discuss in detail the experiences of the Chinese in the United States: Iris Chang's *The Chinese in America* (2003); Arif Dirlik's edited collection *Chinese on the American Frontier* (2001); Madeline Hsu's *The Good Immigrants: How the Yellow Peril Became the Model Minority* (2015); Erika Lee's *At America's Gates* (2003); Jean Pfaelzer's *Driven Out* (2007); and K. Scott Wong and Sucheng Chan's edited collection *Claiming America* (1998).

21. Ironically, this mistrust of the US government in the post-1960s era would be used to justify Asian Americans as the model minority: Asian Americans tend to not ask for social entitlements or go to the police to report crime, leading many to believe that Asians inherited some kind of Confucian spirit that emphasized community over the individual or that they had no crimes in their neighborhoods.

22. Kingston, Maxine Hong, *The Woman Warrior*, 165. All further references to this work will be cited in the text.

23. Chin, "Writing the Other," 89.

24. Ibid.

25. Skenazy, "Coming Home," 108.

26. Hoy, "To Be Able to See the Tao," 62.

27. Ibid., 60.

28. Ibid.

29. Fisher Fishkin, "An Interview," 161.

30. Bonetti, "Interview with Maxine Hong Kingston," 39.

31. Pfaff, "Talk with Mrs. Kingston," *New York Times Book Review*, BR1.

32. Schroeder, "As Truth as Possible," 219.

33. Yang, "Indispensable Labor," 65.

34. Wong, "Staying Alive," 314–15.

35. Blauvelt, "Talking with the Woman Warrior," 84.

36. Mehren, "Dodging Literary Labels," *Los Angeles Times*, 29 April 1991, E1, Web.

37. Strauss, "Simply 'Writer' Will Do," NJ4. To be fair, Chang may be responding to the Tan comparison more than the Kingston comparison, since Tan's work tends to be viewed with decidedly mixed feelings by many Asian American readers as well as writers. See Deanna Fei's "I Called Amy Tan a Dirty Word—and Then She Friended Me" on her website, http://www.deannafei.com/essays/i-called-amy-tan-a-dirty.html.

38. Italie, "Kingston Rises from the Ashes," 13E.

Chapter 2: *The Woman Warrior*

1. For the transcript of President Obama's remarks, see http://www.whitehouse.gov/the-press-office/2014/07/28/remarks-president-presentation-2013-national-medal-arts-and-national-hum.

2. Though there has been no controversy regarding the factual accuracy of *Dreams from My Father*, Obama states outright that he has taken creative license in narrating his coming of age story, blending multiple individuals into one composite character, changing names, compressing timelines. As far as I know, these changes have elicited no criticisms or charges that Obama is "faking" his or his father's Kenyan history, which is not to say of course that Obama has not been labeled a fraud or a fake in multiple other ways.

3. See Fisher Fishkin, "Interview with Maxine Hong Kingston," 782. According to Paul Skenazy and Tera Martin, Maxine Hong Kingston "is the most anthologized of any living American writer, and . . . she is read by more American college students than any other living author" (vii).

4. Michael Krasny, "Interview with Robert Haas," *Forum*, KQED, 22 Aug. 2012, Web.

5. Kang, *Compositional Subjects*, 32.

6. Li, *Imagining the Nation*, 57.

7. In her interview with Shelley Fisher Fishkin conducted in 1989, Kingston notes the fact *The Woman Warrior*, nearly fifteen years after its initial publication, is a perennial trade paperback best seller.

8. Li, *Imagining the Nation*, 57.

9. Of Kingston's critics, the most vociferous over the years has been Frank Chin. The author of plays, novels, and multiple essays, Chin is now best known for these dogged

attacks—often disturbingly personal and hysterical in their ferocity—on Kingston. (David Henry Hwang and Amy Tan have also been targeted by Chin for many of the same reasons as his antipathy toward Kingston, but not to the same degree or intensity.) While the feud between the two is often characterized as an academic debate or philosophical conflict over the nature of Chinese American identity and history, nothing has been written about the threatened violence that often pervades Chin's words against Kingston. In multiple interviews, Kingston has responded to questions regarding the "misunderstanding" between herself and Chin by clarifying that "misunderstanding" is too benign a word to describe their disagreement: Chin has expressed a desire to do violence to her. An interviewer in 1989 prefaces a question toward Kingston with the claim that "Everyone knows that Frank Chin is your most vocal critic and [that he] sort of bothers you," only to have Kingston interrupt him in order to state flatly: "Oh yeah. He threatens me, it's not just bother—he threatens me" (Blauvelt, "Talking with the Woman Warrior," 81). This admission that Chin has threatened her physically elicits no comment from the interviewer. In 1993, Kingston again insists that Chin's critiques cannot be labeled a "misunderstanding" but are rather "attacks." She then informs the interviewer "He even wrote me a letter that he's going to beat me up if he sees me. I don't want to honor him with answers" (Seshachari, "Reinventing Peace," 202). That same year, Kingston repeated this story, telling Donna Perry, "Frank does terrible things. He tells me when he sees me at a conference he's going to beat me up. And I don't answer it because I keep thinking I'm transcending, I'm not being reactive. But then sometimes people see this as weakness and say 'See, these women don't have an answer.' But we don't want to answer because any little thing we do to them will destroy their manhood even worse because they are already so fragile" (Perry, "Maxine Hong Kingston," 184). Chin's threats of physical violence, which I had never been aware of until researching this book, and the fact that Kingston is constantly paired with him—if not in the minds of her readers then certainly within academic circles—is disturbing. For too long, Chin's critiques have played an outsized role in Kingston criticism especially given how debunked, challenged, and misguided that criticism now seems to be. Perhaps Chin should be consigned to the textual space where he belongs—a footnote—to stop giving a spotlight to a writer whose only method of disagreeing with a woman is to threaten to punch her in the face. One must acknowledge the critical history that surrounded and even at times produced Kingston's career, but one does not need to pay deference to it "ad infinitum," especially since most of it is misogynistic, bullying, and even violent in nature.

10. Qtd. in Li, *Imagining the Nation*, 49.

11. Ibid.

12. Johnson, "Ghosts," 19.

13. Qtd. in Li, *Imagining the Nation*, 50.

14. Ibid., 49.

15. Fong, "An Open Letter/Review," 67.

16. Ibid., 68.

17. Cheung, *Articulate Silences*, 77.

18. Ibid.

19. Kingston, "Cultural Mis-readings by American Reviewers," 63; qtd. in Li, *Imagining the Nation*, 53.

20. Ibid., 56.

21. Ibid., 58.

22. Ibid.

23. Kingston also finds it amusing that so many reviewers—many of whom are based on the East Coast—seem to think that all Chinese people live in and around San Francisco, a mistake that Kingston thinks is based on "New York provincialism" ("Cultural Mis-readings," 60).

24. Kingston, "Cultural Mis-readings," 56.

25. Ibid., 57.

26. See, for example, Cheung, "The Woman Warrior versus the Chinaman Pacific," 234–51.

27. Cheung, *Articulate Silences*, 77.

28. Qtd. in Grice, *Maxine Hong Kingston*, 19.

29. Horton, "Interview with Maxine Hong Kingston," 11.

30. Mandelbaum, "Rising from the Ashes," 48.

31. Ibid., 49.

32. Ibid.

33. Kubota, "Maxine Hong Kingston," 2.

34. Qtd, in Li, *Imagining the Nation*, 51.

35. Li, *Imagining the Nation*, 51.

36. Ibid., 52.

37. Bonetti, "Interview with Maxine Hong Kingston," 37.

38. Rabinowitz, "Eccentric Memories," 75.

39. Islas and Yalom, "Interview with Maxine Hong Kingston," 30.

40. Bonetti, "Interview with Maxine Hong Kingston," 33.

41. Skenazy, "Kingston at the University," 119.

42. Ibid., 134.

43. Skenazy, "Kingston at the University," 133. As someone who has always taught and approached *The Woman Warrior* as a work of fiction (with some autobiographical elements), I put a lot of stock in this statement from Kingston. What is more, it is conspicuously true: despite the fact that Kingston could have easily given her narrator a name—her own name—she chose not to do so. It is for these reasons that throughout this volume, I do not refer to the narrator of *The Woman Warrior* or *China Men* as "Maxine" as some other critics have done.

44. Fisher Fishkin, "An Interview with Maxine Hong Kingston," 161.

45. Chu, "The Invisible World the Emigrants Built," 96.

46. Lee, "The Poetics of Liminality and Misidentification,"184.

47. Lee, 185

48. Song, *The Children of 1965*, 64.

49. Hutcheon, *The Politics of Postmodernism*, 22.

50. Ibid., 157.

51. Cheung, "The Woman Warrior v. the Chinaman Pacific," 239.

52. Row, "*The Woman Warrior* at 30."

53. Smith, *Writing Tricksters*, 35.

54. Li, "The Naming of a Chinese American 'I,'" 499.

55. Morante, "From Silence to Song," 78.

56. Ninh, *Ingratitude*, 57.

57. Schueller, "Questioning Race and Gender Definition," 423.

Chapter 3: *China Men*

1. Lee, *Multicultural American Literature*, 33.
2. Chiu, "Being Human in the Wor(l)d," 190.
3. Ling, *Narrating Nationalisms*, 110.
4. Horton, "Interview with Maxine Hong Kingston," 5.
5. Leonard, "Books of the Times: *China Men*," C9.
6. Ibid.
7. Rubenstein, "Myth, Fantasy by a Superb Storyteller," 3.
8. Quan, "Bringing Alive Patriarchal Chinese Enigmas," S6.
9. Ling, *Narrating Nationalisms*, 110.
10. Gordon, "Mythic History," 1.
11. White, "Murmurs of Ancestral Voices," 3.
12. Sabine, *Maxine Hong Kingston's Broken Book of Life*, 2.
13. Pfaff, "Talk with Mrs. Kingston," 15.
14. Qtd in Sabine, *Maxine Hong Kingston's Broken Book of Life*, 1.
15. Perry, "Maxine Hong Kingston," 175.
16. Cheung, *Articulate Silences*, 76.
17. Pfaff, "Talk with Mrs. Kingston," 15–16. Ironically, at the time of *China Men*'s publication, Kingston did not know the full extent of her father's attempts to enter the United States. As she told Paul Mandelbaum, "I finished writing *China Men* and years later [my mother] says: 'Oh, your father stowed away three times on that ship from Cuba to New York. They threw him in jail and deported him, and he got on another ship. He did it three times before he could land.' Why didn't she tell me that earlier? That's much more dramatic and interesting than the way I wrote it, which is that he did it once" (51). Mandelbaum notes that Kingston's work "thrives on the vagaries of memory, translation, and point of view" but that she nevertheless is "vexed" when inaccuracies are discovered after the fact. His point here is that a desire for fidelity to source material on Kingston's part suggests that *China Men* should be read as memoir rather than fiction. This moment can be read in the opposite way however; Kingston is irritated that she could not make her story even more dramatic and difficult than what she assumed to be the truth at the time of composition. One gets the sense that Kingston wishes that she had thought of the idea of making her father enter three times, whether or not it was based in reality.
18. Bonetti, "Interview with Maxine Hong Kingston," 38.
19. Huntley, *Maxine Hong Kingston*, 122.
20. Roorbach, "Maxine Hong Kingston," 167.
21. Pfaff, "Talk with Mrs. Kingston," 15.
22. Lim, "Interview with Maxine Hong Kingston," 159.
23. Chuh and Shimakawa, "Adjudicating Asian America," 29.
24. Ibid.
25. Nishime, "Engendering Genre," 69.
26. Yang, "Indispensable Labor," 65.
27. Cheung, "The Woman Warrior versus the Chinaman Pacific," 240.
28. Shih, "Exile and Intertextuality in Maxine Hong Kingston's China Men," 68.
29. Roorbach, "Maxine Hong Kingston," 169.

30. See http://web.stanford.edu/group/chineserailroad/cgi-bin/wordpress/faqs/ for more historical information on the Chinese and the Transcontinental Railroad. For more historical information on the Chinese and the railroad, see Chang, *The Chinese in America: A Narrative History* and Dirlik, *Chinese on the American Frontier*.

31. Robert Swartout, "Kwantung to Big Sky: The Chinese in Montana, 1864–1900," Chinese on the American Frontier, ed. Arif Dirlik (Lanham, Maryland: Rowman and Littlefield Publishers, 2001), 370.

32. Chiu, "Being Human in the Wor(l)d," 196.

33. Lee, "The Railroad as Message," 278.

34. Okihiro, *Margins and Mainstreams*, 152.

35. Li, "*China Men*: Maxine Hong Kingston and the American Canon," 492

36. Hutcheon, *The Politics*, 77.

Chapter 4: *Tripmaster Monkey*

1. Kakutani, "Goodbye Minimalists, C15.

2. Gold, "Meet Maxine Hong Kingston's Chinese American Beatnik," 349; Leonard, "Of Thee Ah Sing," 768.

3. Chin, "Interview with Maxine Hong Kingston," 58.

4. Leonard, "Of Thee Ah Sing," 768.

5. Ibid.

6. Mukherjee, "Wittman at the Golden Gate," X1.

7. Kakutani, "Being of Two Cultures," C30.

8. Chin, "Interview with Maxine Hong Kingston," 57.

9. Tyler, "Manic Monologue," 46.

10. Mackin, "Split Infinities," 516.

11. Ibid.

12. Kingston, *Tripmaster Monkey*, 29. All further references to this work will be cited in the text.

13. Maini, "Writing the Asian American Artist," 246.

14. Tanner, "Walt Whitman's Presence," 62.

15. Ibid., 65.

16. Alan Trachtenberg, "The Politics of Labor and the Poet's Work: A Reading of 'A Song for Occupations," in *Walt Whitman: the Centennial Essays*, ed. Ed Folsom (Iowa City: University of Iowa Press, 1994), 130.

17. Cyrus Patell, "Representing Emergent Literatures," *American Literary History* 15.1 (2003): 62.

18. Blauvelt, "Talking with the Woman Warrior," 77.

19. Mackin, "Split Infinities," 513.

20. Ibid., 528.

21. Chu, "*Tripmaster Monkey,* Frank Chin," 122.

22. Ibid., 134.

23. Chu, "*Tripmaster Monkey*, Frank Chin," 135.

24. Ibid., 128.

25. Ibid., 129.

26. Smith, *Writing Tricksters*, 57

27. Horton, "Interview with Maxine Hong Kingston," 11.

28. Furth, "Bee-e-een!,"35.

29. Huntley, *Maxine Hong Kingston*, 156.
30. Chang, "Gender Crossing," 16; Leonard, "Of Thee Ah Sing," 768.
31. Hutcheon, *A Poetics*, 4.
32. Ibid.
33. Ibid.
34. Hutcheon, *A Poetics*, 1.
35. Shostak, "Maxine Hong Kingston's Fake Books," 68.
36. Ibid.
37. Chu, "*Tripmaster Monkey*, Frank Chin," 117.
38. Maini, "Writing the Asian American Artist," 43.
39. Wang, "Kingston's Postmodern Representation of a New 'China Man," 101.
40. Cheung, *Articulate Silences*, 77.
41. Mackin, "Split Infinities," 518.
42. Narcisi, "Wittman's Transitions," 95
43. Lee, "I Will Make of My Scaffold a Stage," 127.
44. Banerjee, "The Asian American in a Turtleneck," 65.

Chapter 5: *Hawai'i One Summer, The Fifth Book of Peace,* and *Veterans of War, Veterans of Peace*

1. Kington released *Through a Black Curtain* in 1987 as a "keepsake" book for the Friends of the Bancroft Library at the University of California at Berkeley. This volume, however, contained selections from her previously published works (*The Woman Warrior* and *China Men*) as well as excerpts from her then forthcoming novel, *Tripmaster Monkey*, which would not be published until 1989. As this volume, a limited edition, contained no new written materials from Kingston, I have chosen not to count it as a separate book.
2. Kingston, *Hawai'i One Summer, 1987*, xii. All further references to this work will be cited in the text.
3. Man, "Aloha, Vietnam," 1085.
4. Ibid., 1086.
5. Ibid.
6. Term for the ancient Hawaiian code for laws and regulation.
7. Hawaiian term for Asian Americans from the mainland.
8. Hawaiian term for someone who is local.
9. San Juan Jr., "Dialectics of Aesthetics and Politics," 189.
10. Shulman, "*The Fifth Book of Peace.*"
11. Whalen-Bridge, "The Engaged Aesthetics," 207.
12. Kingston, *The Fifth Book of Peace*, 51. All further references to this work will be cited in the text.
13. Hsu, "Writing, Event, and Peace," 103.
14. Ibid., 104.
15. Ibid.
16. See Blauvelt, "Talking with the Woman Warrior," 80.
17. Lowe, "The Power of Culture," 5.
18. Kingston, *Veterans of War, Veterans of Peace*, 1. All further references to this work will be cited in the text.

Chapter 6: *To Be the Poet* and *I Love a Broad Margin to My Life*

1. Kingston, *To Be the Poet*, 9. All further references to this work will be cited in the text.

2. "*To Be the Poet*," *Publisher's Weekly.com*, 19 Aug. 2002, Web.

3. Orr, "Maxine Hong Kingston's Life in Verse."

4. Rustin, "Maxine Hong Kingston: Singing along with Whitman."

5. Desai, "Review of Maxine Hong Kingston's *I Love a Broad Margin to My Life*."

6. Kingston, *I Love a Broad Margin to My Life*, 3. All further references to this work will be cited in the text.

7. Skenazy, "Kingston at the University," 119.

SELECTED BIBLIOGRAPHY

Books Written or Edited by Maxine Hong Kingston

Kingston, Maxine Hong. *China Men*. New York: Alfred A. Knopf, 1980.

———. *The Fifth Book of Peace*. New York: Knopf, 2003.

———. *Hawai'i; One Summer, 1978*. 1987. Honolulu: University of Hawai'i Press, 1998.

———. *I Love a Broad Margin to My Life*. New York: Alfred A. Knopf, 2011.

———. *Through the Black Curtain*. Berkeley: The Friends of the Bancroft Library, University of California, Berkeley, 1987.

———. *To Be the Poet*. Cambridge, MA: Harvard UP, 2002.

———. *Tripmaster Monkey: His Fake Book*. New York: Alfred A. Knopf, 1989.

———. *The Woman Warrior: Memoirs of a Girlhood Among Ghosts*. New York: Alfred A. Knopf, 1976.

Kingston, Maxine Hong, ed. *Veterans of War, Veterans of Peace*. Kihei, Hawai'i: Koa, 2006.

Essays and Articles by Maxine Hong Kingston

Kingston, Maxine Hong. "Captivated by a Magic Wave." *New York Times*, 26 July 1979: C1.

———. "Cultural Misreadings by American Reviewers." In *Asian and Western Writers in Dialogue: New Cultural Identities*, edited by Guy Amirthanayagam, 55–65. London: Macmillan, 1982.

———. "Duck Boy." *New York Times Magazine*, 12 June 1977: 54–55. Print.

———. "I Choose the Poet's Life: Maxine Hong Kingston Invites the Muse." *The Woman's Review of Books* 19, no. 10–11 (2002): 5.

———. "Imagined Life." *Michigan Quarterly Review* 22, no. 4 (1983): 561–71.

———. "Let Freedom Ring in China." *Los Angeles Times*, 4 July 1989: 61. *Proquest*. Web. 24 Aug. 2015.

———. "A Letter to Garret Hongo upon the Publication of the Open Boat." *Amerasia Journal* 20.3 (1994): 25–26.

———. "The Making of More Americans." *The New Yorker*, 11 Feb. 1980: 34–42. Print.

———. "The Novel's Next Step." *Mother Jones* 14, no. 10 (1989): 37–41.

———. "Opening Speech." In *The Legacy of Maxine Hong Kingston*, edited by Sami Ludwig and Nicoleta Alexoae-Zagni, 21–29. Zurich: LIT Verlag, 2014.

———. "Reservations about China." *Ms.* Oct. 1978: 67–68. Print.

———. "Rupert Garcia: Dancing between Realms." *Mother Jones* 32, no. 8 (1988): 32–35.

———. "San Francisco's Chinatown: A View from the Other Side of Arnold Genthe's Camera." *American Heritage* 30 (Dec. 1978): 36–47.

———. "Talk Story: No Writer Is an Island—Except in Hawai'i." *Los Angeles Times,* 4 June 1978: S3. Print.

———. "Violence and Non-Violence in China, 1989." *Michigan Quarterly Review* 24 (1990): 62–67.

———. "A Writer's Notebook from the Far East." *Ms.* Jan. 1983: 85–86. Print.

Documentaries or Videos Featuring Maxine Hong Kingston

Kingston, Maxine Hong. *Stories My Country Told Me with Maxine Hong Kingston.* Films for the Humanities and Sciences: Princeton, NJ, 2000. Video.

———. *The Stories of Maxine Hong Kingston.* Films for the Humanities and Sciences: Princeton, NJ, 1994. Video.

———. *Maxine Hong Kingston: Talking Story.* CrossCurrent Media: San Francisco, CA, 1990. Video.

Interviews of Maxine Hong Kingston

Carabí, Angels. "Interview with Maxine Hong Kingston." *Atlantis* 10, no. 1–2 (1988): 139–46.

Blauvelt, William Satake. "Talking with the Woman Warrior." In *Conversations with Maxine Hong Kingston,* edited by Paul Skenazy and Tera Martin. Jackson: University Press of Mississippi, 1998, 77–85.

Bonetti, Kay. "Interview with Maxine Hong Kingston (1986)." In *Conversations with Maxine Hong Kingston,* edited by Paul Skenazy and Tera Martin. Jackson: University Press of Mississippi, 1998, 33–46.

Brownmiller, Susan. "Susan Brownmiller Talks with Maxine Hong Kingston, Author of *The Woman Warrior.*" In *Maxine Hong Kingston's* A Woman Warrior*: A Casebook,* edited by Sau-ling C. Wong, 173–180. New York: Oxford UP, 1999.

Chin, Marilyn. "An Interview with Maxine Hong Kingston." *MELUS* 16, no. 4 (1989–1990): 57–74.

Fisher Fishkin, Shelley. "An Interview with Maxine Hong Kingston." *American Literary History* 3, no. 4 (1991): 782–91.

Horton, Karen. "Interview with Maxine Hong Kingston." In *Conversations with Maxine Hong Kingston*, edited by Paul Skenazy and Tera Martin, 5–13. Jackson: University Press of Mississippi, 1998.

Hoy, Jody. "To Be Able to See the Tao." In *Conversations with Maxine Hong Kingston,* edited by Paul Skenazy and Tera Martin, 47–66. Jackson: University Press of Mississippi, 1998.

Islas, Arturo, and Marilyn Yalom. "Interview with Maxine Hong Kingston." In *Conversations with Maxine Hong Kingston*, edited by Paul Skenazy and Tera Martin, 21–32. Jackson: University Press of Mississippi, 1998.

Jaggi, Maya. "The Warrior Skylark." In *The Guardian Online.* The Guardian. 13 Dec. 2003: Web. 9 July 2015.

Kubota, Gary. "Maxine Hong Kingston: Something Comes Outside Onto the Paper." In *Conversations with Maxine Hong Kingston*, edited by Paul Skenazy and Tera Martin, 1–4. Jackson: University Press of Mississippi, 1998.

Lim, Shirley Geok-lin Lim. "Reading Back, Looking Forward: A Retrospective Interview with Maxine Hong Kingston." *MELUS* 33, no. 1 (2008): 157–70.

Mandelbaum, Paul. "Rising from the Ashes: A Profile of Maxine Hong Kingston." *Poets and Writers Magazine* 26, no. 3 (1998): 46–53.

Martin, Michel. "Maxine Hong Kingston Takes Pride in Mixed Heritage." *Tell Me More*. NPR.org. 4 July 2007. Web. 21 July 2015.

"Maxine Hong Kingston after the Fire." *Powells.com*. Powell's Books, 10 Oct. 2006. Web. 3 August 2015.

Mills, Kay. "Literature by the Lode and by Lore." *Los Angeles Times Online*. Los Angeles Times. 25 Aug. 1985: Web. 8 July 2015.

Moyers, Bill. "Maxine Hong Kingston." *Bill Moyers Journal*. PBS.org. 25 May 2007. Web. 8 July 2015. Transcript.

Perry, Donna. "Maxine Hong Kingston." In *Conversations with Maxine Hong Kingston*, edited by Paul Skenazy and Tera Martin, 168–88. Jackson: University Press of Mississippi, 1998.

Pfaff, Timothy. "Talk with Mrs. Kingston." *New York Times Book Review,* 15 June 1980: BR1, 25, 26. Print.

Rabinowitz, Paula. "Eccentric Memories: A Conversation with Maxine Hong Kingston." In *Conversations with Maxine Hong Kingston*, edited by Paul Skenazy and Tera Martin, 67–76. Jackson: University Press of Mississippi, 1998.

Reed, Josephine. "Maxine Hong Kingston Discusses Her Path-Breaking Books." *Arts.gov*. National Endowment for the Arts, 10 May 2012. Web. 30 June 2015.

Schroeder, Eric. "As Truth as Possible: An Interview with Maxine Hong Kingston." In *Conversations with Maxine Hong Kingston*, edited by Paul Skenazy and Tera Martin, 215–28. Jackson: University Press of Mississippi, 1998.

Seshachari, Neila. "Reinventing Peace: Conversations with Tripmaster Maxine Hong Kingston." In *Conversations with Maxine Hong Kingston*, edited by Paul Skenazy and Tera Martin, 192–214. Jackson: University Press of Mississippi, 1998.

Skenazy, Paul. "Kingston at the University." In *Conversations with Maxine Hong Kingston*, edited by Paul Skenazy and Tera Martin, 118–58. Jackson: University Press of Mississippi, 1998.

Skenazy, Paul, and Tera Martin, ed. *Conversations with Maxine Hong Kingston*. Jackson: University of Mississippi Press, 1998.

Thompson, Phyllis Hoge. "This Is the Story I Heard: A Conversation with Maxine Hong Kingston and Earll Kingston." *Biography* 6, no. 1 (1983): 1–12.

Ulin, David. "The Writer's Life: Maxine Hong Kingston Picks Up the Story." *Los Angeles Times Online*. Los Angeles Times. 2 Feb. 2011: Web. 8 July 2015.

Whalen-Bridge, John. "A Conversation with Charles Johnson and Maxine Hong Kingston." *MELUS* 31, no. 2 (2006): 69–93.

Zagni, Nicoleta Alexoae. "An Interview with Maxine Hong Kingston." *Revue française d'études américaines* 110 (2006): 97–106.

Profiles and Popular Articles

Guthrie, Julian. "Maxine Hong Kingston Embarks on New Life Chapter." *SF Gate.com*. Hearst Communications, Inc. 23 Jan. 2011. Web. 20 Sept. 2015.

Italie, Hillel. "Kingston Rises from the Ashes." *The Victoria Advocate*. 28 Dec. 2001, 13E. Print.

Iwata, Edward. "Word Warriors." *Los Angeles Times Online*. Los Angeles Times. 24 June 1990: Web. 8 July 2015.

Loke, Margaret. "The Tao Is Up." *New York Times*, 30 Apr. 1989: SM 28. *Proquest*. Web. 24 Aug. 2015.

Mehren, Elizabeth. "Dodging Literary Labels." *Los Angeles Times*, 29 April 1991: E1. *Proquest*. Web. 24 Aug. 2015.

———. "Nine Writers on the Eve of a China Adventure." *Los Angeles Times*, 24 Oct. 1984: H1. *Proquest*. Web. 24 Aug. 2015.

Mills, Kay. "By Lode and By Lore." *Los Angeles Times*, 25 Aug.1985: G3. *Proquest*. Web. 24 Aug. 2015.

Robertson, Nan. "'Ghosts' of Girlhood Lift Obscure Book to Peak of Acclaim." *New York Times*, 12 Feb. 1977: 26. Print.

Row, Jess. "*The Woman Warrior* at 30: Maxine Hong Kingston's Secrets and Lies." *Slate.com*. Slate Group, 27 Mar. 2007. Web. 3 Aug. 2015.

Smith, Lynn. "Author Mixes Ying, Yang in Her Writing." *Los Angeles Times*, 27 Apr. 1986: OC-D1. *Proquest*. Web. 24 Aug. 2015.

Yardley, Jonathan. "*Woman Warrior* [*sic*]: A Memoir that Shook the Genre." *Washington Post Online*. Washington Post. 19 June 2007: Web. 3 Aug. 2015.

Reviews of Kingston's Published Works

Desai, Manan. "Review of Maxine Hong Kingston's *I Love a Broad Margin to My Life*." *Hyphen Magazine*. n.p., 8 June 2011. Web. 15 Oct. 2015.

Fong, Katheryn. "An Open Letter/Review." *Bulletin of Concerned Asian Scholars* 9, no. 4 (1977): 67–69.

Gold, Herbert. "Far-Out West: Meet Maxine Hong Kingston's Chinese-American Beatnik." *Chicago Tribune*, 16 Apr. 1989: 349. *Proquest*. Web. 24 Aug. 2015.

Gordon, Mary. "Mythic History." *New York Times Book Review*, 15 June 1980: 1, 24. Print.

Johnson, Diane. "Ghosts." *New York Review of Books*, 3 Feb. 1977: 19–21.

Kakutani, Michiko. "Being of Two Cultures and Liking and Loathing It." *New York Times*, 14 Apr. 1989: C30. *Proquest*. Web. 24 Aug. 2015.

———. "Goodbye Minimalists: Hello Tellers of Tales." *New York Times*, 31 May 1989: C15. *Proquest*. Web. 24 Aug. 2015.

Kramer, Jane. "On Being Chinese in China and America." *New York Times Book Review*, 7 Nov. 1976: 1, 18, 20. Print.

Leonard, John. "Books of the Times: *China Men*." *New York Times Online*. New York Times. 3 June 1980: Web. 24 Aug. 2015.

———. "In Defiance of Two Worlds." *New York Times*, 17 Sept. 1976: C21. Print.

———. "Of Thee Ah Sing." *The Nation* 5 June 1989: 768–72. Print.

Mardenfeld, Sandra. "Review of *Hawai'i One Summer*." *New York Times*, 14 Feb 1999: BR21. *Proquest*. Web. 24 Aug 2015.

Mukherjee, Bharati. "Wittman at the Golden Gate." *Washington Post*, 16 Apr. 1989: X1. Print.

Orr, David. "Maxine Hong Kingston's Life in Verse." *New York Times Online*. New York Times, 3 Mar. 2011: Web. 21 July 2015.

Quan, Phyllis. "Bringing Alive Patriarchal Chinese Enigmas." *Los Angeles Times*, 22 June 1980: S6. *Proquest*. Web. 24 Aug. 2015.

Rubenstein, Roberta. "Myth, Fantasy by a Superb Storyteller." *Chicago Tribune Book World* 23 June 1980: 3, 7. *Proquest*. Web. 24 Aug. 2015.

Rustin, Susana. "Maxine Hong Kingston: Singing along with Whitman." *The Guardian Online*. The Guardian. 26 Apr. 2011: Web. 15 Oct. 2015.

Shulman, Polly. "Out of the Ashes." *New York Times Online*. New York Times. 28 Sept. 2003: Web. 3 Aug. 2015.

"To Be a Poet." *Publisher's Weekly.com*. PWxyz LLC. 19 Aug. 2002. Web. 22 Nov. 2015.

Tyler, Anne. "Manic Monologue." *The New Republic* 17 Apr. 1989: 44–46. Print.

Vizenor, Gerald. "The Triumph of Monkey Business." *Los Angeles Times*, 23 Apr. 1989: L1. *Proquest*. Web. 25 Aug. 2015.

White, Edmund. "Murmurs of Ancestral Voices." *Washington Post Book World* 22 June 1980: 3. *Proquest*. Web. 24 Aug. 2015.

Critical and Secondary Sources

Allen, Joseph R. "Dressing and Undressing the Chinese Woman Warrior." *positions* 4, no. 2 (1996): 343–79.

Arthur, Jason. "The Chinatown and the City: Kingston, Kerouac, and the Bohemian Bay Area." *MFS: Modern Fiction Studies* 58, no. 2 (2012): 239–60.

Banerjee, Mita. "The Asian American in a Turtleneck: Fusing the Aesthetic and the Didactic in Maxine Hong Kingston's *Tripmaster Monkey*." In *Literary Gestures: The Aesthetic in Asian American Writing*, edited by Rocio G. Davis and Sue-Im Lee, 55–69. Philadelphia: Temple UP, 2006.

Begum, Khani. "Confirming the Place of 'The Other': Gender and Ethnic Identity in Maxine Hong Kingston's *The Woman Warrior*." In *New Perspectives on Women and Comedy*, edited by Regina Barreca, 143–56. Philadelphia: Gordon and Breach, 1992.

Bolacki, Stella. "'It Translated Well': The Promise and Perils of Translation in Maxine Hong Kignston's *The Woman Warrior*." *MELUS* 34, no. 4 (2009): 39–60.

Chan, Stephanie. "'Refusing Food': Asian Pacific American Eaters in the World as Pedagogical Example." *Asian American Literature: Discourses and Pedagogies* 2 (2011): 30–37.

Chang, Hsiao-Hung. "Gender Crossing in Maxine Hong Kingston's *Tripmaster Monkey*." *MELUS* 22, no. 1 (1997): 15–34.

Cheng, Anne Anlin. *The Melancholy of Race: Psychoanalysis, Assimilation, and Hidden Grief*. New York: Oxford UP, 2001.

Cheung, King-Kok. *Articulate Silences: Maxine Hong Kingston, Joy Kogawa, and Hisaye Yamamoto*. Ithaca: Cornell UP, 1993.

———. "'Don't Tell': Imposed Silences in *The Color Purple* and *The Woman Warrior*." *PMLA* 103, no. 2 (1988): 162–74.

———. "Talk-Story: Counter-Memory in Maxine Hong Kingston's China Men." *Tamkang Review: A Quarterly of Comparative Studies Between Chinese and Foreign Literatures* (Taipei) 24, no. 1 (1993): 21–37.

———. "The Woman Warrior versus the Chinaman Pacific: Must a Chinese American Critic Choose between Feminism and Heroism?" In *Maxine Hong Kingston's* The Woman Warrior*: A Casebook*, edited by Sau-ling Cynthia Wong, 113–34. New York: Oxford UP, 1999.

Chiu, Monica. "Being Human in the Wor(l)d: Chinese Men and Maxine Hong

Kingston's Reworking of *Robinson Crusoe*." *Journal of American Studies* 34, no. 2 (2000): 187–206.

Chu, Patricia. "'The Invisible World the Emigrants Built': Cultural Self-Inscription and the Antiromantic Plots of *The Woman Warrior*." *Diaspora: A Journal of Transnational Studies* 2, no. 1 (1992): 95–15.

———. "*Tripmaster Monkey*, Frank Chin, and the Chinese Heroic Tradition." *Arizona Quarterly* 53, no. 3 (1997): 117–39.

Chuh, Kandice, and Karen Shimakawa. "Adjudicating Asian America." In *The Cambridge Companion to Asian American Literature*, edited by Daniel Kim and Crystal Parikh, 29–43. New York: Cambridge UP, 2015.

Chun, Gloria. "The High Note of the Barbarian Reed Pipe: Maxine Hong Kingston." *Journal of Ethnic Studies* 19, no. 3 (1991): 85–94.

Crawford, Danielle. "'Vinegar Soup Improved His Womb': Food, Appetite, and the Redefining of Asian American Masculinity in Kingston's *China Men*." *Asian American Literature: Discourses and Pedagogies* 4 (2013): 63–75.

Dirlik, Arif, ed. *Chinese on the American Frontier*. Lanham, Maryland: Rowman and Littlefield, 2001.

Dong, Lan. *Mulan's Legend and Legacy in China and the United States*. Philadelphia: Temple University Press, 2011.

Eakin, John Paul. *Fictions in Autobiography: Studies in the Art of Self-Invention*. Princeton: Princeton UP, 1985.

Eng, David. *Racial Castration: Managing Masculinity in Asian American Literature*. Durham: Duke UP, 2001.

Fong, Bobby. "Maxine Hong Kingston's Autobiographical Strategy in *The Woman Warrior*." *Biography* 12, no. 2 (1989): 116–26.

Furth, Isabella. "Bee-e-een! Nation, Transformation and the Hyphen of Ethnicity in Kingston's *Tripmaster Monkey*." *MFS: Modern Fiction Studies* 40, no. 1 (1994): 33–49.

Goellnicht, Donald. "Father Land and/or Mother Tongue: The Divided Female Self in Kogawa's *Obasan* and Hong Kingston's *The Woman Warrior*." In *Gender and Genre in Literature: Redefining Autobiography in Twentieth Century Women's Fiction*, edited by Janice Morgan and Colette Hall. New York: Garland Publishing Inc., 1991, 119–34.

———. "Tang Ao in America: Male Subject Positions in China Men." In *Reading the Literatures of Asian America*, edited by Shirley Geok-lin Lim and Amy Ling, 191–212. Philadelphia: Temple UP, 1992.

Goldman, Marlene. "Naming the Unspeakable: The Mapping of Female Identity in Maxine Hong Kingston's *The Woman Warrior*." In *International Women's Writing: New Landscapes of Identity*, edited by Anne E. Brown and Marjanne E. Gooze, 223–32. Westport, CT: Greenwood Press, 1995.

Grice, Helena. *Maxine Hong Kingston*. Manchester, UK: Manchester UP, 2006.

Griffiths, Jennifer. "Uncanny Spaces: Trauma, Cultural Memory and the Female Body in Gayl Jones's *Corregidora* and Maxine Hong Kingston's *The Woman Warrior*." *Studies in the Novel* 38, no. 3 (2006): 353–70.

Gsoels-Lorensen, Jutta. "Impossibilized Subjects in Maxine Hong Kingston's *China Men*: Thoughts on Migrancy and the State of Exception." *Mosaic* 43, no. 3 (2010): 103–18.

Hattori, Tomo. "China Man Autoeroticism and the Remains of Asian America." *NOVEL: A Forum on Fiction* 31, no. 2 (1998): 215–36.

———. "Psycholinguistic Orientalism in Criticism of *The Woman Warrior* and *Obasan*." In *Other Sisterhoods: Literary Theory and US Women of Color,* edited by Sandra Kumamoto Stanley, 119–38. Urbana: University of Illinois Press, 1998.

Hsu, Shounan. "Writing, Event, and Peace: The Art of Peace in Maxine Hong Kingston's *The Fifth Book of Peace*." *College Literature* 37, no. 2 (2010): 103–24.

Huntley, Edelma D. *Maxine Hong Kingston: A Critical Companion.* Westport, CT: Greenwood Press, 2000.

Hutcheon, Linda. *A Poetics of Postmodernism: History, Theory, Fiction.* London: Routledge, 1988.

Kang, Laura, *Compositional Subjects: Enfiguring Asian/American Women.* Durham: Duke University Press, 2002.

———. *The Politics of Postmodernism.* London: Routledge, 1989.

Kim, Elaine. "Visions and Fierce Dreams: A Commentary on the Works of Maxine · Hong Kingston." *Amerasia* 8, no. 2 (1981): 145–61.

Lee, A. Robert. *Multicultural American Literature: Comparative Black, Native, Latino/a and Asian American Fictions.* Edinburgh: Edinburgh University Press, 2003. 20–36.

Lee, Christopher. *The Semblance of Identity: Aesthetic Mediation in Asian American Literature.* Stanford: Stanford UP, 2012.

Lee, Julia H. "The Railroad as Message in Maxine Hong Kingston's *China Men* and Frank Chin's 'Riding the Rails with Chickencoop Slim.'" *The Journal of Asian American Studies* 18, no. 3 (2015): 265–87.

Lee, Katherine. "The Poetics of Liminality and Misidentification: Winnifred Eaton's *Me* and Maxine Hong Kingston's *The Woman Warrior*." In *Transnational Asian American Literature: Sites and Transits*, edited by Shirley Geok-Lin Lim, John Blair Gamber, Stephen Sohn, and Gina Valentino, 181–96. Philadelphia: Temple UP, 2006, 181–96.

Lee, Sun Hee Teresa. "'I Will Make of My Scaffold, a Stage': Performing the Asian American Subject in Maxine Hong Kingston's *Tripmaster Monkey: His Fake Book*." *MELUS* 38, no. 3 (2013): 126–45.

Lee, Yoon Sun. "Kingston's China Men: Circumscribing the Romance of Deterritorialization." *Yale Journal of Criticism* 11, no. 2 (1998): 465–84.

———. "Type, Totality and the Realism of Asian American Literature." *Modern Language Quarterly* 73, no. 3 (2012): 415–32.

Li, David Leiwei. "*China Men*: Maxine Hong Kingston and the American Canon." *American Literary History* 2, no. 3 (1990): 482–502.

———. *Imagining the Nation: Asian American Literature and Cultural Consent.* Stanford: Stanford UP, 1998.

———. "The Naming of the Chinese American 'I': Cross-Cultural Sign-ifications in *The Woman Warrior*." *Criticism* 30, no. 4 (1988): 497–515.

Lim, Jeehyun. "Cutting the Tongue: Language and the Body in Kingston's *The Woman Warrior*." *MELUS* 31, no. 3 (2006): 49–65.

Lim, Shirley Geok-lin. "*The Woman Warrior*: Her Planetary Asian American Imagination." *American Book Review* 31, no. 1 (2009): 4–5.

Lin, Patricia. "Clashing Constructs of Reality: Reading Maxine Hong Kingston's *Tripmaster Monkey: His Fake Book* as Indigenous Ethnography."In *Reading the*

Literatures of Asian America, edited by Shirley Geok-lin Lim and Amy Ling, 110–38. Philadelphia: Temple UP, 1992.

Ling, Jinqi. *Narrating Nationalisms: Ideology and Form in Asian American Literature*. New York: Oxford UP, 1998.

Lowe, John. "Monkey Kings and Mojo: Postmodern Ethnic Humor in Kingston, Reed, and Vizenor." *MELUS* 21, no. 4 (1996): 103–26.

Ludwig, Sami, and Nicoleta Alexoae-Zagni, eds. *On the Legacy of Maxine Hong Kingston*. Zurich: LIT Verlag Münster, 2014.

Mackin, Jonna. "Split Infinities: The Comedy of Performative Identity in Maxine Hong Kingston's *Tripmaster Monkey*." *Contemporary Literature* 46, no. 3 (2005): 511–34.

Madsen, Deborah. "Chinese American Writers of the Real and the Fake: Authenticity and the Twin Traditions of Life Writing." *Canadian Review of American Studies* 36, no. 3 (2006): 257–71.

Maini, Irma. "Writing the Asian American Artist: Maxine Hong Kingston's *Tripmaster Monkey: His Fake Book*." *MELUS* 25, nos. 3–4 (2000): 243–464.

McDaniel, Nicole. "'Remaking the World' One Story at a Time in *The Fifth Book of Peace* and *Veterans of War, Veterans of Peace*." *MELUS* 36, no. 1 (2011): 61–81.

Melchior, Bonnie. "A Marginal 'I': The Autobiographical Self Deconstructed in Maxine Hong Kingston's *The Woman Warrior*." *Biography* 17, no. 3 (1994): 281–95.

Miller, Margaret. "Threads of Identity in Maxine Hong Kingston's *Woman Warrior* [*sic*]." *Biography* 6, no. 1 (1983): 13–33.

Morante, Linda. "From Silence to Song: The Triumph of Maxine Hong Kingston." *Frontiers: A Journal of Women's Studies* 9, no. 2 (1987): 78–82.

Myers, Victoria. "The Significant Fictivity of Maxine Hong Kingston's *The Woman Warrior*." *Biography* 9, no. 2 (1986): 112–25.

Narcisi, Lara. "Wittman's Transitions: Multivocality and the Play of *Tripmaster Monkey*." *MELUS* 30, no. 3 (2005): 95–111.

Ninh, erin Khuê. *Ingratitude: The Debt-Bound Daughter in Asian American Literature*. New York: New York UP, 2011.

Nishime, Leilani. "Engendering Genre: Gender and Nationalism in *China Men* and *The Woman Warrior*." *MELUS* 20, no. 1 (1995): 67–82

Oishi, Eve. "The Asian American Fakeness Canon, 1972–2002." *Aztlan: A Journal of Chicano Studies* 32, no. 1 (2007): 197–204.

Okihiro, Gary. *Margins and Mainstreams: Asians in American History and Culture*. Seattle: University of Washington Press, 1994.

Rabine, Leslie. "No Lost Paradise: Social Gender and Symbolic Gender in the Writings of Maxine Hong Kingston." *Signs* 12, no. 3 (1987): 471–92.

Roorbach, Bill. "Maxine Hong Kingston." In *American Writers: A Collection of Literary Biographies V*, edited by Jay Parini, 157–175. New York: Charles Scribner's Sons, 2000.

Royal, Derek Parker. "Literary Genre as Ethnic Resistance in Maxine Hong Kingston's *Tripmaster Monkey: His Fake Book*." *MELUS* 29, no. 2 (2004): 141–56.

Sabine, Maureen. *Maxine Hong Kingston's Broken Book of Life: An Intertextual Study of* The Woman Warrior *and* China Men. Honolulu: University of Hawai'i Press, 2004.

San Juan, Jr., E. "Dialectics of Aesthetics and Politics in Maxine Hong Kingston's *The Fifth Book of Peace*." *Criticism* 51, no. 2 (2009): 181–209.

Sato, Gayle K., "Reconfiguring the 'American Pacific': Native Reenactments of Viet Nam in Maxine Hong Kingston's *The Fifth Book of Peace*." *The Japanese Journal of American Studies* 16 (2005): 111–33.

Schueller, Malini. "Questioning Race and Gender Definitions: Dialogic Subversions in *The Woman Warrior*." *Criticism* 31, no. 4 (1989): 421–37.

Shan, Te-Hsing. "Life, Writing, and Peace: Reading Maxine Hong Kingston's *The Fifth Book of Peace*." *Journal of Transnational American Studies* 1, no. 1 (2009): 1–22.

Shapiro, Elliott. "Authentic Watermelon: Maxine Hong Kingston's American Novel." *MELUS* 26, no. 1 (2001): 5–28.

Shaw, Jonathan. "'A Lot You Know about Us Monkeys': Representation and Reference in Kingston's *Tripmaster Monkey: His Fake Book*." *MELUS* 36, no. 1 (2011): 177–94.

Shih, Shu-mei. "Exile and Intertextuality in Maxine Hong Kingston's *China Men*." In *The Literature of Emigration and Exile*, edited by James Whitlark and Wendell Aycock, 65–78. Lubbock, Texas: Texas Tech University Press, 1992.

Shostak, Debra. "Maxine Hong Kingston's Fake Books." In *Critical Essays on Maxine Hong Kingston*, edited by Laura Skandera-Trombley, 51–76. New York: Hall, 1998.

Shu, Yuan. "Cultural Politics and Chinese-American Female Subjectivity: Rethinking Kingston's *Woman Warrior* [*sic*]." *MELUS* 26, no. 2 (2001): 199–223.

Sledge, Linda Ching. "Maxine Hong Kingston's *China Men*: The Family Historian as Epic Poet." *MELUS* 7, no. 4 (1980): 3–22.

Slowik, Mary. "When the Ghosts Speak: Oral and Written Narrative Forms in Maxine Hong Kingston's *China Men*." *MELUS* 19, no. 1 (1994): 73–88.

Smith, Jeanne. "Rethinking American Culture: Maxine Hong Kingston's Cross Cultural *Tripmaster Monkey*." *Modern Language Studies* 26, no. 4 (1996): 71–81.

———. *Writing Tricksters: Mythic Gambols in American Ethnic Literature*. Berkeley: University of California Press, 1997.

Smith, Sidonie. "Filiality and Women's Autobiographical Storytelling." In *Maxine Hong Kingston's* The Woman Warrior*: A Casebook*, edited by Sau-ling Cynthia Wong, 57–82. New York: Oxford UP, 1999.

Song, Min. *The Children of 1965: On Writing, and Not Writing, as an Asian American*. Durham: Duke UP, 2013.

Tanner, James. "Walt Whitman's Presence in Maxine Hong Kingston's *Tripmaster Monkey: His Fake Book*." *MELUS* 20, no. 4 (1995): 61–74.

Williams, A. Noelle. "Parody and Pacifist Transformations in Maxine Hong Kingston's *Tripmaster Monkey: His Fake Book*." *MELUS* 20, no. 1 (1995): 83–100.

Wong, Sau-ling. "Autobiography as Guided Chinatown Tour? Maxine Hong Kingston's *The Woman Warrior* and the Chinese American Autobiographical Controversy." In *Maxine Hong Kingston's* The Woman Warrior*: A Casebook*, edited by Sau-ling Cynthia Wong, 29–53. New York: Oxford UP, 1999.

———. Introduction to *Maxine Hong Kingston's* The Woman Warrior*: A Casebook*, edited by Sau-ling Wong. New York: Oxford UP, 1999, 3–16.

———. *Reading Asian American Literature: From Necessity to Extravagance*. Princeton: Princeton UP, 1993.

———. "Staying Alive: Kingston's *The Woman Warrior* Afterlife and Marilyn Chin's *Revenge of the Mooncake Vixen*." In *The Legacy of Maxine Hong Kingston*, edited by Sami Ludwig and Nicoleta Alexoae-Zagni, 313–342, Zurich: LIT Verlag, 2014.

Woo, Deborah. "Maxine Hong Kingston: The Ethnic Writer and the Burden of Dual Authenticity." *Amerasia* 16, no. 1 (1990): 173–200.

Wu, Qing-Yun. "A Chinese Reader's Response to Maxine Hong Kingston's *China Men.*" *MELUS* 17, no. 3 (1991–1992): 85–94.

Yang, Caroline. "Indispensable Labor: The Worker as a Category of Critique in *China Men.*" *MFS: Modern Fiction Studies* 56, no. 1 (2010): 63–89.

Zackodnik, Teresa. "Photography and the Status of Truth in Maxine Hong Kingston's *China Men.*" *MELUS* 22, no. 3 (1997): 55–69.

INDEX